SOUL
BEGINNINGS

8 Strategies for Overcoming Life's Challenges

Shellie Anderson-Tazi

BERKLEY BOOKS, NEW YORK

While the author has made every effort to provide accurate telephone numbers and Internet addresses at the time of publication, neither the publisher nor the author assumes any responsibility for errors or for changes that occur after publication.

B

A Berkley Book
Published by The Berkley Publishing Group
A division of Penguin Group (USA) Inc.
375 Hudson Street
New York, New York 10014

PRINTING HISTORY
Berkley trade paperback edition / October 2004

Library of Congress Cataloging-in-Publication Data

Anderson-Tazi, Shellie.
Soul beginnings : eight strategies for overcoming life's challenges / by Shellie Anderson-Tazi.
p. cm.
Includes bibliographical references.
ISBN 0-425-19822-7
1. Health behavior. 2. Medicine, Preventive. 3. Self-realization. 4. Survival skills.
I. Title

RA776.9.A53 2004
158.1—dc22   2004046318

PRINTED IN THE UNITED STATES OF AMERICA

10 9 8 7 6 5 4 3 2 1

I dedicate this book and prayer to my entire family. May God bless us all with perfect health. Please, Lord, look after my family and give us the knowledge to be emotionally and physically content. Allow us to love at all times, forgive at all times, and have the courage to change for the sake of serving you.

Contents

CONTENTS

Foreword

I first met Shellie when I spoke at her college, Bowie State. When she approached me, I remember her being an incredible force of light. I could probably count on one hand the number of people who have really stood out in those kinds of environments—and she was one of them. She has a unique energy that's hard to miss. Somehow she becomes the friend you never had, but always wanted.

So Shellie just inserted herself into my life. I don't know how that came to be but it was a joy. She is a joy. I really wish I could paint a picture of how our lives became so intertwined. But I guess when something feels as natural as our friendship does, the details don't really matter. What does matter is that every time there was a major event going on in my life, Shellie was there to lend her support. For instance, when my apartment was recently renovated, it was Shellie who helped me move. Or when my cousin was dying from cancer, Shellie supported my family through those tough times. And once when I was really in a funk, and I couldn't even articulate it, Shellie saw right through me. "Come, let's do this," she offered. Before I knew it, we were visiting the kids that I'd adopted at the group home. I don't know what was actually bothering me but whatever it was, the feeling just dissipated. Hanging out with Shellie confirmed what I'd known in my spirit: When you are in a funk, you can transform your spirit by stepping outside of yourself and doing something for someone else. Shellie has a way of keeping me connected to the things that I hold dear and she continues to be a rock in my life. I know there is nothing that she wouldn't do for me. There aren't a lot of people who get who I am and are able to respond to me in a way that helps keep me going. Shellie is the exception. I know that I can count on her and consider her a really good friend.

The fact is, we're not running buddies or anything like that. Our friendship is not one that sustains itself through frequent contact. But it's a very deep, powerful friendship, and I feel a great sense of comfort just knowing that she is there.

When Shellie was diagnosed with cancer, I was able to be there for her. She's my friend, she needed my help, and I was doing what came natural to me. Anyone who knows me knows that I'm always connecting people. I knew the limits to the extent of my outreach during her challenging time, but I also knew my mom and aunt, who also live in Mount Vernon, New York, could nurture her. She needed a strong support system. So I made the connection. I passed on everything that I came across about breast cancer that I thought would help her understand what she was going through and let her know that she could get through this. And, yes, the deluge of information I directed her way was nonstop. I read everything. So this allowed me to help her in the most supportive way that I could, given that I was trying to run a business.

And true to form, Shellie, even in the midst of battling cancer, continued to be a blessing. But at this time, she probably didn't even realize how much of an inspiration for me she'd actually become. Her ability to shine in the face of adversity was, and continues to be, admirable. On the day she was diagnosed with cancer, she was only twenty-nine years old and her husband just up and left. Can you imagine? Events like that would cripple the average person. But after she dried her tears, she came through it like a champ. She recognized her challenge and then started strategizing ways she could move forward. "I have cancer; I want to live," she concluded. Then she devised a plan. Beyond that, she had the faith and courage to act on her plan. Instead of wallowing in her pain, which probably would have been very understandable, she looked at the hand she was dealt and played to win. Later she saved her life and spirit and inspired others by helping them to become more physically fit. Shellie is a prime example of how someone can overcome challenges with grace, courage, and dignity. That's what I admire in her. All of us go through things and, by the grace of God, we get through them but I'm not sure if I would have gotten through that kind of experience with such courage and grace.

Shellie also helped me to see her cancer as a blessing, not a curse. Most people understand that cancer has the power to take a life, but rarely can it be said to provide the extraordinary power to transform a life positively. Blessings have a way of disguising themselves. Cancer gave Shellie a new perspective. I see her greater confidence. Prior to her illness, Shellie didn't know how phenomenal she was. She was just doing what she did and didn't have a clue of her true potential. Although she has always been a go-getter, now she exudes even greater self-assurance. I've been encouraging her to tell her story and create opportunities to do so, and that has helped her become more aware of her influence. But since she's had cancer, I think she realizes how people respond to her, and she knows that she has a real gift that she needs to share.

I'm not trying to paint a picture of a saint here. But Shellie's qualities are too important and too special to miss. Her light, her smile, her presence, and her spirit draw you like a moth to light. And really, it's not about Shellie. It's not even her. People are responding to the God force within her. We are all here on this earth to do God's work, and she accepts her special assignment from him with joy and commitment. Her earthly duty is to take her gifts and challenges and use them to help other people get through their lives. And she's doing an amazing job. I'm so proud of her.

But you don't have to take my word for it. Read her words for yourself. I don't think there is anyone who won't be touched—transformed even—after hearing Shellie's story and getting to know her life. You will believe that no matter what you're going through, you'll not only come through it but you'll claim victory in the end. Life is funny that way; sometimes it requires that we understand and appreciate another person's story in order for us to heal our own pain.

Know that God's plan is unfolding for you just the way it is supposed to. And may the powerful truth you learn from Shellie and her story live in your spirit and help you learn to heal your life. Continue to stay strong and share your magnificent light.

Terrie Williams

Preface

A Word to My Children

Dear Amir:

My love, I write this book in hopes that you will grow and know that you are a true prince. You are born to make a dramatic impact on the world. Sorry for putting such a burden on you, but I was born to make that same mark and I am doing that by making a difference in the lives of others and writing this book.

You were given to me and your father as a gift from God. As a baby, you changed our lives and no longer did we ever question God's purpose or love. We now know that he loves us unconditionally and that between the two of us being Muslim and Christian, God still shows his favor on our lives. We pray together and know that there is only one God.

All of your grandparents are alive: Malika and Ahmed Tazi, Brenda and Robert Anderson, and even your great grandmother Lillie M. Green. I haven't seen a day yet that they are not praying for me, you, and Daddy.

You will be faced with a lot of challenges in this life. Remember where your parents and grandparents are from and the pain that they must have endured. Yet still they loved and honored God. Remember to stay prayerful and always love because it conquers all.

I love you.
Mommy

To the two children of mine who didn't survive before and while writing this book, I love you with all my heart. While mourning your lives, I am constantly reminded of why it's important to write this book about facing and overcoming challenges. My prayer is that my loss will be someone else's gain.

To my child that is on the way, I thank God for your coming into existence while writing this book. I love you, and I pray that you will become an awesome light in the universe. As you grow in me, I am reminded that I should never give up on my dreams, because your existence proves that dreams do come true. I asked God to bless me with another child and he is sending you.

Thank you, Lord, for loving and trusting Abdeltif and me with another one of your blessings.

With love,
Mommy

Introduction

I'd just signed a publishing deal for a book intended to tell women how they can overcome the various tragedies they encounter in their lives. Besides overcoming the challenge of maneuvering myself through the unfamiliar world of book publishing, I first had to figure out whether I was ready to expose myself to the public. To make matters worse, I'm thinking about this dilemma from a hospital bed—I've just experienced yet another tragedy.

It all started a few days ago, when I decided to take a pregnancy test after a bout of nausea. I was elated when I found out that I was pregnant. The problem was that when I went to the gynecologist for an examination, she told me that she couldn't see the fetus in my uterus on the sonogram. As a result, she directed me to get blood work. While waiting for the results at my home, I started feeling contractions and my husband rushed me to the emergency room. It turned out that I had an ectopic pregnancy, a condition in which the fertilized ovum implants itself on any tissue other than the endometrial lining of the uterus. In my case, my baby was caught in my right fallopian tube. When the doctors proceeded to operate, they discovered that the right tube had ruptured, causing a pint of blood to settle in my pelvic area. They couldn't understand how I was still living. In any case, they ended up removing the entire tube, and I'm left trying to pick up the pieces left of my life—once again.

The drastic chain of events that have shaped my life up until this point started nine years ago. In the midst of an argument with my ex-husband (we were married at that time), I went into premature labor. He ran out of the house. At the time, I thought he was just leaving me to fend for myself but I later found out he went to call an ambulance. By the time I arrived at the hospital, the baby's feet were hanging out. I delivered a girl weighing only one pound, three ounces. I passed out upon seeing her. When I woke up, she was gone. I was left behind wondering how God could take my precious daughter away. I couldn't eat, and it seemed as if my tears would never stop falling. Her father wanted no part of the situation. I felt alone and was very confused about how my life was going. Besides that, I still had a child to bury and no money to do it. At the funeral home, it took me an hour just to get myself to stop crying. I was numb as I told the funeral director to have my daughter cremated, mostly because that was the only alternative we could afford.

Nine months following her death, I found a small lump in my right breast. It was no larger than a pearl earring. When I went to the doctor's office to get it checked out, they assumed the lump was some milk left behind from my recent pregnancy. Still, they suggested outpatient surgery to remove the lump for further diagnosis. Two weeks later, I received a call from my doctor, asking me to come into the office to discuss the findings of the tests. I thought it was just routine. After all, the doctors had already assured me that I didn't have anything to worry about.

My husband and I entered her office expecting her to tell me that everything was okay. Maybe she'd suggest that I lose weight or cut down on my cholesterol. When I sat down, however, the doctor blurted out that I had breast cancer. They had found cancerous cells when the lump was removed. Everything after that moment is a blur. I'm sure she explained everything to us because we stayed in her office for two hours so she could respond to our questions and concerns. But I went blank. The only thing that she said that was crystal clear was that my young age—at that time, I was only twenty-nine years old—was even more cause for concern because the cells multiply faster in younger people. I didn't know exactly what that meant as far as my own circumstances were concerned, but I did understand that the news wasn't good at all.

Now you'd think that after I was diagnosed with breast cancer, my day couldn't have gotten any worse. Think again. When my husband and I parked the car in front of our apartment, he confessed that my new diagnosis was more than he could handle. To ease his stress, he told me that he would pack his things in the morning and leave. Just like that.

The walls came tumbling down. When I finally got the strength to climb the stairs, enter my apartment, and enter my living room, I fell to my knees and howled. I screamed as if my heart were breaking, because it was. I screamed as if my life depended on it, because it did.

To say that I was scared is an understatement. I was in the Big Apple with very few friends and only distant family. At the time that I was diagnosed with cancer, my mom was living in Maryland. My husband of two years was abandoning me. I was alone and dying. What next?

I picked up the phone and dialed the number of my godmother, Marie. I was so upset that I was hyperventilating, and she could barely understand anything I was saying. "Where are you?" she asked.

"Home."

"Can you get to where I am?" she probed.

"Yes," I sobbed.

I slumped in my car with puffy eyes and running nose and raced over to Marie's house. When I arrived, Marie was talking on the phone and she handed me the receiver. The woman on the other end told me that she had also been diagnosed with cancer. "You'll be fine," assured Francis Wynn.

I tried to act as graciously as I could under the circumstances, but I really wanted to let this stranger on the phone know that she didn't have a clue. Obviously, she hadn't heard the doctor tell me that I would surely die and that time was short.

My friend stroked me and told me to cry as much as I wanted. She showed her love for me and allowed me to express my pain. At some point we decided to call my mom and the antics really began. As usual, Mom was her dramatic self. In fact, she was so dramatic that it was hard for me to stay focused on my own problems. She offered to come up and stay with me. But I assured her that it was best if she stayed put. I knew she really couldn't afford the sudden relocation, and I thought that I would have had to console her because the news hit her pretty hard. In hindsight, it seems she probably would have been the support that I needed.

Life was very hard. Besides finding out that I was losing a husband and going to die, I also had to make decisions about what treatments I should choose to try to extend my days as long as possible. The choices seemed dismal at best. According to the doctors, chemotherapy and radiation were the treatments of choice. But I wondered why I should even listen to them, since it was a doctor who initially told me I didn't have anything to worry about. Besides, the prospect of putting poison in my veins to turn into a bald-headed scarecrow didn't seem at all appealing—even if it was going to help me live longer. Besides, it was common knowledge that chemo made you sterile. What kind of life would I have?

As far as I was concerned, chemotherapy was out. But one of my friends was convinced that chemotherapy was exactly what I needed to save my life. To allay my fears, this can't-take-no-for-an-answer friend of mine promised to stay by my side the entire time when I did my first bout of chemo. The offer was nice, but I refused. Then one evening she met me at Barnes & Noble and read a five-page letter that she believed was divinely inspired. She told me that after she prayed for my life, God gave her a message to write that would motivate me to want to live. She believed He was speaking through her so that He could reach me. Her letter included things about my life that I'd never told her or anyone else. It mentioned things in my childhood that she couldn't have possibly known. She also told me about past mistakes and included some key things about how bitter I'd become because of the resentment I held against others. Most important, she encouraged me to forgive myself so that I could move on. "God loves you," she insisted. "And he's going to use this tragedy for good."

By the end of our conversation, I was in tears. She made me realize that I needed to take measures to live if I was ever going to claim victory. Finally, I agreed to start chemotherapy treatments.

Was chemo as bad as I thought it would be? It was worse. I was tired, very tired. The chemo made me feel like I was losing my mind. I was delusional. I was lonely. I was emotionally drained. I was sick. I was nauseous. I was sleep-deprived. Despite my illness, I got up every morning and went to work at the Society of Motion Pictures and Television Engineers (SMPTE). It's no wonder: What else did I have? I didn't have much family in New York City and my husband had abandoned me. Somehow, my work made me feel as if I was still doing at least one thing that mattered.

Just as my doctor warned, my hair started to fall out. So this same *pushy* girlfriend (thank God, she never took no for an answer) convinced me to participate in every woman's favorite pastime—shopping. We were on the hunt for the perfect wig and, after some exploration, we located it at this fly wig shop in Queens, New York. There had to be three hundred wigs in that shop and I attempted to sport them all. My girlfriend urged me to purchase a long wig that hung down my back and ended somewhere around my behind. I tried it on but felt totally ridiculous, because it made me look like a fake Diana Ross. Next, I struck a pose in a semilong wig that hung past my shoulders and decided to pass on that as well. And then I spotted it. Off in the corner was the most beautiful mushroom-shaped braid wig that I'd ever seen. This was a wig beyond wigs, and when I put it on, it moved and really stood out. I hadn't seen anyone with that kind of wig before. After trying it on, I knew that was the wig for me and was glad I'd taken the trip to Queens.

Even with my fabulous wig, however, my hair loss made me feel as if I'd turned into an alien. But once I accepted that my hair was truly all gone, I had a chance to see the real me. All the hair I used to have on my head prevented me from seeing my almond-shaped eyes, my full lips, and my button nose. Despite the cancer, I was beautiful.

It was the strangest thing. Prior to my bout with baldness, I never really thought I was particularly attractive. But when I looked deep into my eyes I could see the real me. The one that my mother loved and the one that my godmother embraced. For the first time in my life, I liked my physical appearance.

From that point on, my life became more manageable—even enjoyable, in some instances. Cancer introduced me to things I'd never even fathomed and reintroduced me to many of my past loves. Take aerobics, for example. One day a colleague asked me if I would go with her to aerobics class, since she knew I was a former aerobics instructor. I declined. The next day she asked me again. I declined again. But her persistent invitations broke me down, and finally I accepted. Exercise not only made me feel physically better, it boosted my mood.

That first session was probably the best workout I'd ever had. Instead of being tired, I was invigorated. I thoroughly enjoyed the experience and inspired the other students to step up their workout as well. The instructor was so impressed that she later called me to ask if I would teach an aerobics class for fifteen dollars a session. The cash, even though nominal, was the incentive that I needed to seal the deal. And once I began dancing, I was working it. The more I moved, the more I wanted to move because I noticed that the sick feeling that I'd had from the chemo was disappearing. The bitter taste in my mouth was fading. The students were impressed, to say the least. They were totally caught off guard by my energy and enthusiasm. They expected an easy class but I surprised them. At 250 pounds, I was dancing like a woman half my size. I couldn't help it, the music was good and I felt great. Those first five students turned into fifty in two months. Good news spreads fast.

Eventually, I had so many students that I had to expand my hours. So I taught a 6:00 A.M. class prior to going to work as well as a 6:30 P.M. class. Lives were being changed in that aerobics class. Women with various issues joined in, even though they initially thought they didn't have a shot at fitness. They simply followed my lead. We all learned to live in those classes because our workout was followed by intense rap sessions. Since my friend Marie is a social worker, I'd ask her for insight on how to advise some of the women in my class. The students appreciated the insight but the experience was doing more for me than I could have ever predicted. After I started teaching aerobics, I didn't have any more complications from chemo. Who would have thought that aerobics could mean so much to so many people?

And just as my friend promised months earlier, God started to use my tragedy for good. Through aerobics I was helping others heal. My class of fifty multiplied into much larger classes, television appearances, radio interviews, and magazine articles. I taught aerobics to anyone who wanted healing and that sometimes took me out of the state and over the airwaves. Several organizations recognized me for the impact I was having on women's lives. But my quest has never been for recognition. My cancer forced me to appreciate life and I was compelled to share that message with others. And the message was not just for breast cancer survivors but for anyone who was struggling to overcome a life-changing blow. Not only was I a breast cancer survivor, I was a survivor who had overcome the death of a child, my own divorce, the divorce of my parents when I was ten years old, as well as other calamities, before age thirty.

More blessings followed. As it turned out, my ex-spouse's swift departure made room for a new love. I met Abdelitif Tazi while I was getting my chemotherapy treatments. This man loves me unconditionally, the way God loves me. Even though he knew that there was a possibility I couldn't have children, he asked me to marry him anyway. On November 27, 1999, we were wed. It was held in the heart of North Carolina, because my Dad had just gotten out of the hospital and was unable to travel. We had nine groomsmen, seven bridesmaids, and a host of guests. Though the festivities were held during the Thanksgiving season, God provided us with a beautiful, warm sunny day.

And the predictions about my not being able to have a child were all wrong. Shortly after I got married, my darling son entered the world. Not only did the cancer treatments not make me sterile, they didn't harm my baby, either. Our love child was born without a blemish on May 17, 2000. At ten pounds and five ounces, our bundle of joy was perfect.

God had replenished everything that I'd lost, exceeding my expectations, and beating out all of the predictions.

I've shared this message in various venues including Fox 5's *Good Day New York*, WNBC's *Today Show*, *The View*, *Heart & Soul* magazine, *The Journal News*, *Essence*, *Mode* magazine, WLIB, and CD 101.9. I've been fortunate enough to reach women in all walks of life—white, black, young, and old. Although I believe that I've made a difference in each of these women's lives, my mission is specifically to help African-American women because I share their pain.

But my challenges are in no way over. Right now I'm sitting here bearing the mental and physical hurt that I'm experiencing as a result of another baby that I've lost. Part of me wants to give up. Living the life of a survivor is a hard job. So we—my prayer partner Joyce Kelly, my sister-in-law Zoila Tazi, and myself—are holding hands as we ask for God's mercy during this challenge.

The nurse just walked in. "I read your chart, you have gone through so much at such a young age," she remarked. "You are very strong, so you'll be fine." I wanted to tell her that she was wrong because the feeling of despair that overwhelms my soul might just kill me. Life hurts aren't only painful but they can cause so much fear in your spirit that they can nearly bring you to your knees. But I don't complain. Instead, I struggle to put a smile on my face, because I can't stop thinking about God's goodness—even during these trying times. I am a living witness that God will not give us any more than we can bear. And this calamity provides me with one more opportunity to reaffirm my commitment to letting women know that a life-altering tragedy does not have to be a death sentence and that each of us has the power to overcome any challenge that comes our way. If I can triumph over tragedy, you can too!

Like you, I don't know what the future will hold for me. But I'm certain that I'll always come out a winner as long as I practice eight essential steps, and maintain a positive outlook.

Soul Beginnings: Eight Strategies for Overcoming Life's Challenges will outline an eight-step program that you can refer to from the time you encounter a tragic situation until it's resolved. Using specific examples and illustrations from my own experiences, I will show you how to put winning recovery strategies into play. These techniques will show you how to P.U.S.H. (Pray Until Something Happens), develop a support system, release past hurts, upgrade your exercise program, focus on activities that matter most to you, determine what lessons the tragedy is trying to teach you and develop a solid plan for the future. In addition, the appendices contain specific advice for African-American breast cancer survivors—the largest segment of women who die from this disease. This section provides the signs of breast cancer, a copy of the medical record showing my breast cancer diagnosis, with guidelines on how to read and understand it, a list of resources, physical exercise techniques for breast cancer survivors, and guidelines for selecting the right support group.

But don't expect to enter this journey wearing rose-colored glasses. We're going to keep it real here. Each chapter opens with a page from my journal and reveals the way I was feeling at various times in my life, and things weren't always pretty. Life isn't always pretty but it's livable and lovable as long as you keep stepping up to each challenge with the tools you need to strive and survive.

So let's get started on our path to recovery. We will get through this—together.

Step 1

P.U.S.H.: Pray Until Something Happens

11/16/95

My life is over. Today my doctor told me that I have breast cancer and that I have two to five years to live.

And if that wasn't bad enough, my husband told me it was too much for him to handle and went on his way. That bastard left me. How could you leave your wife on the very day that she finds out that she has cancer? How could you be so cruel?

Damn him! Damn everybody! But I don't know why I'm surprised. Everything we ever had together has been cursed from day one. Just last year I lost a child by him. In the middle of one of our arguments about him not being home enough, I went into labor. I kept telling him that something seemed wrong with me and he walked out on me, leaving me to fend for myself. I struggled to call my doctor, then a major contraction hit me, causing me to drop the phone.

The next thing I knew, the ambulance arrived and rushed me to Mount Vernon Hospital. By the time I got there, the nurse told me that the baby's feet were coming out. My baby was born dead, weighing one pound and three ounces.

Now the first time he left was bad enough. And you'd think, since I forgave him once, he would have behaved differently. But here I am with breast cancer, not knowing if I am going to live or die, and he leaves me again.

What do I do now?

So you've just gotten the news? Don't despair, sis. As the Bible says in Psalm 30:5: "Weeping may last for a night but joy comes in the morning." I didn't always believe that. When I was first diagnosed with breast cancer, one of the first things I did was get on my knees and ask God not to let me die. But then I refined my request, asking for his help, guidance, and mercy so that I could at least get through that one moment in time. And he delivered.

When the next morning came, I realized I was still alive and that gave me another day to fight for my life. From that point on, I'd decided I was going to put up a fight because if I had given up that would mean that I was giving up on myself. Despite my despair, I wasn't ready to give up because, deep inside my heart, I wanted to live. I didn't know why I wanted to live, how I wanted to live, or why I was even alive. But I knew that there was so much more I wanted to do with my life, and I couldn't afford to have it cut short. Breast cancer was in for a battle.

Like me, you may not have devised a master plan as to how you are going to get through this latest tragedy that has crossed your path. That's okay. You can always fill in the details later. The important thing is that you choose survival over despair, the rest will take care of itself as long as you're willing to put some smart practices into play.

Of course, you may be wondering how you develop a game plan

when the whole ordeal caught you by surprise? Just take it one moment at a time. Nobody is ever fully prepared when tragedy strikes, but that doesn't mean you can't overcome it. I know I wasn't prepared for the string of calamities that came my way on March 25, 1995—a date that will be forever etched in my soul. But that date also provided me with the opportunity to make prayer an integral part of my life. Breast cancer forced me to "go through to get through," and I grew in the process.

Like me, you may not think that prayer is necessary, believing that whatever will be will be. Have you been wrong all of your life? Maybe. Prior to my getting breast cancer, I'd spent seven or eight years believing that prayer wasn't something I needed, only to find out that, at times, prayer was the only thing that would truly sustain me.

You need prayer, too.

MATTHEW 7:7–8
Ask and it will be given to you; seek and you will find; knock and
the door will be opened to you. For everyone who asks receives; he
who seeks finds; and to him who knocks, the door will be opened.

When I look back on my life now I can see why breast cancer entered my world. It may sound crazy but I thank God that he not only allowed me to live through that experience but learn from it. The most important thing I took from the experience is that, no matter how grave the circumstance, I know I have a chance as long as I continue to P.U.S.H. (Pray Until Something Happens). By doing that, I demonstrate that I'm no longer trusting in the world or my flesh to influence my life but I'm depending on my connection with God to direct my path. With God's help, I can expect outcomes that I could never have believed possible because I know there is a greater force at work.

So, how do you P.U.S.H.? It really is no different from how we were taught to pray as a child: humble yourself, realize that the Creator is in control of the outcome, and be open for guidance from a source that's outside of yourself. The Bible says that you have not because you ask not. If you want a solution, ask for one. That's what I did. But, of course, you have to believe that a solution exists. And for that, you need faith.

EZRA 8:23
So we fasted and petitioned our God about this, and he answered our prayer.

Speaking of faith, prayer is nothing but a delusion unless you believe wholeheartedly that God (or whatever spiritual force you believe in) will intercede on your behalf. For me, keeping the faith was a challenging process so I did specific things to help me increase it. As an example, I had my pastor pray in my apartment, and I then rearranged the rooms in the house in an attempt to purify the environment around me. I even asked friends to come over and pray in my apartment with me in an attempt to rally up support. Those things are what I needed to be able to put the disaster that was before me underneath my bed and away from my pillow.

But maybe you're not exactly sure what you need. That's okay, because this chapter will help you determine what you need from the spiritual force so that you can pray accordingly. Regardless of your desire—for wisdom, support, a cure, or maybe just the ability to accept the circumstances—we'll take a look at specific guidelines so you can pray for results. We'll consider a number of solutions to help you increase your faith. Beyond that, we'll review some additional resources such as books, Web sites, and counseling services to help you strengthen your faith in prayer. So let's get started.

4

DETERMINING YOUR NEEDS

I CHRONICLES 4:9–10

Jabez was more honorable than his brothers. His mother had named him Jabez, saying, "I gave birth to him in pain." Jabez cried out to the God of Israel, "Oh, that you would bless me and enlarge my territory! Let your hand be with me, and keep me from harm so that I will be free from pain." And God granted his request.

For me, finding out what I needed was taking an honest assessment of the things that I knew was wrong in my life and asking God to help me change them. How did I know which things to pinpoint? Anything that left me with a bad feeling or sour taste in my mouth were the things I knew I needed to change. Instead of settling for feelings of anger, confusion, resentfulness, or vengefulness, I used these emotional conditions as a barometer to determine when I needed prayer. This allowed God to transform those negative feelings into more useful ones. To more fully integrate prayer in your life, take the following steps:

Admit that you need prayer. I thought that implementing prayer in my life would help me forgive—forgive my husband, myself as well as others who I believed had wronged me. Somehow, I thought all of the built-up resentfulness was contributing to my illness, and prayer would be my saving grace. For you, it may be something else that leads you to want prayer in your life. Look at this challenge in your life and what role prayer can play to help you deal with this issue more successfully. Even if you don't know why you need prayer, I ask you to take a leap of faith and just believe that you need it. Sometimes things only make sense in reverse; I guarantee that at some point in the process you will realize why you need prayer.

EZRA 9:6

O my God, I am too ashamed and disgraced to lift up my face to you, my God, because our sins are higher than our heads and our guilt has reached to the heavens.

Transform from victim to victor. As I struggled with breast cancer, which came on the heels of a miscarriage, I initially believed that God had picked me out and given me the bottom of the barrel to work with. I wondered what was wrong with me. And I couldn't understand how life could be so cruel. Now, I know that God was not picking on me at all, at least not in a negative sense. He had chosen me because he knew I could serve as an example of his goodness to others who were experiencing the same challenges that I encountered. It all makes sense. So when things happen at this point in my life, I no longer ask God, "Why me?" Now I say, "Why not me?" Prayer helped me to see that everything happens for a reason, and I focus on the possibilities instead of the problem.

Consider Deborah Cofer's story as a shining example of how you can find the lesson in a truly heartbreaking experience. I met Deborah while participating in a program for women's history month. Recently she had a situation that was so devastating, it literally caused her to collapse. But ultimately, Deborah used the experience to transform her way of thinking:

I got married in June 2003. Two months later, on August 11, my husband told me that he thought he'd made a mistake. He realized he wasn't ready for marriage because he'd had some unresolved issues that he believed would affect the marriage. He saw what wonderful things God planned for me and he didn't want to get in the way. In closing, he told met that I really deserved someone better and on August 16, he walked out of my life.

There had been no discord in the marriage, and he'd never ever communicated that he was having second thoughts, so his departure really came as a shock. I was devastated. The whole experience just baffled me. Nobody seemed to have any answers for why this happened to me and my only way of getting through it was my spiritual connection. I prayed. I asked God for guidance and understanding. It was a hard time. My daughter had just been diagnosed with lupus and was put in the hospital on the same day that my husband made his announcement. Prior to that, I'd left a job making lots of money to chart a new course for myself, but my decision had made it very difficult for me financially.

Then things seem to come to a head. One day, I sat down on my couch and literally couldn't get up. I went into a depression that was so deep that I just emotionally shut down. I felt myself in the midst of this but I couldn't get up off the couch. I kept hearing in my head, "Call for help, you're in crisis." But there was another part of me that thought I could come out of it. Finally, I realized that I really did need help. I wanted to maintain my sanity, so I called my doctor. She told me to get into her office right away. I was in such an emotional state that I was afraid to drive my car or even catch a cab by myself. As I cried hysterically, I called my friend to take me to my doctor, who then put me on an antidepressant. That helped to balance out the emotional trauma that I was going through. Then, I continued to pray and ask God to guide me.

Today, only two months after the whole ordeal, I'm on top of the world again. I feel a sense of strength because of the things that were revealed to me through prayer. Now things make sense. I realized that most of the men in my life have all been carbon copies of one another in some way. Psychologically they were what I needed as a way of protecting myself from the sexual abuse I'd endured as I child. As a result of that disturbing experience, I'd built up a psychological wall that I'd hidden behind so that anytime I became intimate with a man I was unable to see him for who he really was, *for fear that what I saw would be too traumatic for me to deal with. But in essence, the experience of my husband walking out on our marriage after only two months forced that wall to come crumbling down. Before the breakup, I never really looked at my husband. Afterwards, when I looked at him, I saw a sixteen-year-old kid. This was a man who probably had never matured beyond that age, so he wasn't mature enough emotionally to have made a decision about marriage. This experience has made me stronger and more aware of why I made the choices I've made in men.*

But if I hadn't had that spiritual connection, I don't think I would have made it through. Even though the experience was very devastating for me, I am very thankful to have gotten to the other side to receive the blessing that was waiting for me. There are a lot of lessons that we have to go through in life that really strengthen us and prepare us for the rest of our journey. Some of these trials are necessary for our own personal growth and development. The stronger we are, the more capable we are of helping others. There is a lot of pain and people who need to be understood but you can't understand them unless you go through certain things yourself.

Deborah's winning attitude has reshaped her life and you can refer to her example as a source of inspiration.

Think outside the box. *If you always do what you've always done, you'll always get what you've always got.* I know it's a saying that you've heard many times before, so why not listen? The bottom line: If you want things to turn out differently, you need to make some changes. I suggest putting yourself in places that you don't usually frequent. For me, I surrounded myself with wise women. These older women helped me determine that I was on the wrong path. I sought their advice and in some cases I took heed. It paid off. Sometimes thinking outside of the box meant that I had to put myself in awkward situations with others (like attending family outings I once skipped), so I could find my true self. For you, it could mean making amends with someone that wronged you or just familiarizing yourself with people you've never allowed yourself to know. Think about what things you're going to do differently to impact the outcome of your current circumstance. Prayer can help you see options that you never considered; don't be afraid to open up.

Focus on others. That seems almost crazy, right? You'd think that if you're the one going through a tragedy, then the solution would come by focusing on you. But that isn't necessarily so. I've found that serving others (even when my free time was at a premium) did more for me than focusing on my troubles. Why? Because changing my focus enabled me to see how fortunate I really was when I saw other people's struggles. Instead of sulking about my own pain, I counted my blessings and offered prayers of thanksgiving. You, too, will develop an attitude of gratitude once you start helping others in need.

Implement the three Ps. To prompt my transformation, I implemented Prayer, Patience, and a Process. Here's how you can use them for your recovery:

Pray before you do anything. Now at the time I started this, it was all new because I didn't consider myself a spiritual person. I thought people who were into prayer were the holy rollers who wore crosses and preached on the subway. But, once I began to see how my prayers got results, then it wasn't hard for me to start praying about everything, including which clothes I picked out each day, who I spoke to on the telephone, where I drove my car, and how I behaved on my job with my coworkers. I also prayed for people like my family, friends, and coworkers. Each time I prayed, I realized it provided me with a positive outlook. So, let me pass this advice on to you: Pray as much as you can whenever you can. Pray when you need to resolve a conflict with someone, consider gossiping about your peers, think negatively about your circumstance, or are angry, upset, or annoyed. You should even pray when you're happy, so you can show your appreciation for God's grace and blessings. And you don't always have to ask for a miracle. Sometimes I just ask God to look after me and protect me from evil. It's just that simple. I meditate on what it is that I need from the Creator, drop to my knees, or look up to the heavens to plead my case.

Patience may be a virtue, but for me, it has been a challenge. I wasn't patient because I thought I deserved to get my way, or I resented doing something that I really didn't want to participate in. Additionally, my impatience also came from feeling guilty about not doing the things that made other people happy. I was obsessed with being a people pleaser, but now I realize my happiness does not have to depend on the happiness of others. Tragedy forced me to discover how I could better handle my responses to the situations in my life and it has become much easier for me to exercise patience. The wait has become much shorter since I stopped watching the clock.

The *process* is the mechanism that puts a plan into play. Prior to my transformation, I'd always wanted to do things quickly without any thought about the process. That didn't work. A lot of things didn't get finished and even when tasks were finished, they weren't done correctly. But once I paid more attention to the process, I was better able to reach my goals—both personally and professionally. So I caution you, sis, don't throw caution to the wind, and don't ignore the process that's required to get things done. Maybe there is a waiting period—certain tests that need to be taken, or particular objectives that need to be met—before you can proceed to the next level. That's okay. Do what needs to be done, so you can get where you have to go. Shortcuts could cost you precious time and force you to backtrack to do things that could have been done a long time ago.

So I say, forge ahead with the process that you need to get the desired results.

Life coach Paula McGee, president of Paula McGee Ministries, a nonprofit organization whose vision is to "inspire every woman to recognize, accept, and fulfill her call to greatness" discovered that the three Ps—prayer, patience, and process—were critical when she was going through a challenging time in her life.

September 11 is a day that most Americans will remember as one of deep heartache. September 11 was one day; however another date— May 16 of the same year—claimed my attention. On that day my mother suffered a major stroke. A normal morning changed with one phone call from my twin sister stating that my mother was in the emergency room. With a race to the airport, a plane ride, and a rental car journey, I was at the hospital in the Intensive Care Unit. Monitors and tubes everywhere caught my family's attention as we prayed and watched the doctors and nurses work diligently to keep my mom alive. Each day we sat at her bedside, with her unable to speak or recognize any of us. It was one of the most painful situations in my life. I felt overwhelming powerlessness.

Each day was another challenge and another decision. Each decision was critical to her life. I fought through the anger and, most of all, the fear—the fear that I would lose my mother as suddenly and without preparation as I'd lost my father. I had to work through the fear, remain open to make decisions, and help my siblings. It was difficult, but I kept working to sow quiet time and self-care. Self-care meant fighting for time. My siblings and I handled the trauma and the shock in our own unique way. Each of us, based on our personality, birth order, and fears, responded differently. Self-care meant my refusing to spend the night at the hospital when my siblings insisted that was the only appropriate sacrifice and response. I tried to honor their wishes to keep the peace and maintain my childhood role as the peacemaker. But, the hospital robbed me of sleep. The tension was too great for me to rest in an unfamiliar environment. Without sleep, I was unable to make the critical decisions about my mother's health. Self-care meant stealing a few moments every day in front of my laptop to write my book and to even dare to write about including a time for deep pain and suffering. I fought through the guilt of writing a book—investing in my dreams—when my mother was fighting to regain her life and control of her body. Writing was my attempt to establish balance. The writing gave me a moment of escape from a very painful time.

Whenever we are faced with this level of pain and suffering, we can seek what the Creator is teaching us through the experience, and look for deeper healing. We can choose to see these unexpected and painful occurrences as an opportunity to meet the Creator in a deeper place, to find a fresh start, and a unique way of being in the world. Those days in the intensive care unit and the months that followed had a great impact on everyone involved. Throughout the experience, I learned compassion. Watching my mother bravely face each physical challenge and obstacle—watching her valiant attempts to learn to do all of the little things that we take for granted—I learned patience. Sitting with her when nurses and attendants dressed her and fed her, I learned the true meaning of dignity.

I also learned something that they never taught me in seminary. I learned that I could not dictate a time schedule or a list of appropriate gifts from the Creator. I learned that I am responsible for the sowing, but the Creator produces the harvest. Each day at her bedside, sometimes fighting back my own tears, I learned to be thankful for each gift, each harvest—even the gifts that I often took for granted and overlooked, like my mother's laughter. I reaped the harvest of time and its true value. I no longer take any days for granted. I know how to slow down and wait—to trust the Creator and honor each small movement and each small blessing. Most important,

I have learned always to sow in faith—to be intentional about self-care—and to cherish my dreams. I learned how to sow into them, especially at the times when they seem the most elusive.

When we are strategically working on what we sow, especially in difficult times, we will begin to change. We will move to a better place away from the patterns that prevent us from growing.

As Paula's story illustrates, the three Ps are essential when dealing with a challenge.

Be honest. It's important to tell the truth to people so you allow yourself to get the proper treatment, whatever form that may take. Breast cancer and the death of my child forced me to examine my lifestyle and take responsibility for the results. There were times in my life, particularly after I was diagnosed with breast cancer, when it seemed as though there were dark shadows even when the sun was out. Darkness was not only on the inside of me but darkness also surrounded me because of my negative thoughts and bad company. By being honest and prayerful, I found that I was living my life for the wrong reasons, and that helped me change some of my ways.

Be humble. A humble heart is an attractive heart. You can't expect God or anyone else to help you with your situation if you cop an attitude. Know that the challenge of understanding why you need prayer only comes with a lot of giving in and being humble. Now being humble doesn't mean you're a wimp, sucker, or loser. On the contrary, if I wanted to win, I had to lose the negativity that often came with being aggressive, miserable, forceful, rude, and downright mean. Humbleness requires a strong person who is willing to force their instincts to take a backseat to let the righteousness of their heart step to the forefront. When I learned to do this, I actually liked myself better because I developed a warm, relaxed, sensitive spirit. And with this

I realized that my life was a gift and that in itself is a humbling experience.

Let God. Part of implementing prayer in your life means that you've made the choice to let God intercede on your behalf. It means you are giving up control of the situation to a more powerful force. After you've prayed about a situation, believe that God has already worked it out. Take my friend D. G. Wilson Davis, for instance. According to her, prayer got her the results she needed for healing. "When I was diagnosed with cancer, I asked to be healed and suffer no pain," she recalls with conviction in her voice. "Twelve years later, I'm still healed and in no pain. Praise God!" Don't just pray for prayer's sake, pray for results.

THESSALONIANS 5:16–18
Be joyful always. Pray continually. Give thanks in all circumstances,
for this is God's will for you in Christ Jesus.

PRAYING FOR RESULTS

So now you've determined what you need so you have a sense of what to pray for. But your prayer won't do you any good unless you know how to pray for results. I found that praying for results forced me to acknowledge that God was in control and He was working it out for me. I first had to have an honest heart and believe that God existed. Then I had to get to work. Here are some things *you* need to do to make some good things happen.

Fess up. In determining your needs, I suggested that you be honest. But if you want results you have to be honest with yourself and God. That means you need to confess your sins and ask for forgiveness intending to exchange those bad habits for more positive ones.

Read, write and recite. "People sometimes forget that they can pray for answers because they get so bogged down with an issue or problem by trying to figure it out for themselves. You need to ask God what he thinks about this," suggests Valorie Burton, life coach and author of *Listen to Your Life: Following Your Unique Path to Extraordinary Success,* who says she sometimes communicates with God by writing Him a letter. I definitely suggest that you write your prayer requests down on paper. Read them on a daily basis so that you become familiar with them. As your prayers are answered, cross them off the list and add more. During my tragedies, I acknowledged when my prayers were being answered. And I didn't want to miss out on the simple things in life by focusing only on the spectacular. I was just as grateful for the opportunity to see a blue sky as I was when my cancer went into remission. As far as I am concerned, all of God's blessings are worth celebrating.

Make prayer a habit. It's important to pray on a regular basis at a specific time. Every day, at the same time I would pray. I would also ask others to pray for me at that specific time. This prevented me from feeling alone in my walk through trying times. Constant prayer also forced me to be accountable for my part in the results and ensured that God was provided with an open invitation on a daily basis. It really brought me closer to what his plan was for my life. And when negativity arose, as it often does, praying on a regular basis gave me the opportunity to ask God to intervene on my behalf and that often helped me shape a more positive outcome for the rest of the day. Constant contact with God allowed me to refuel on a regular basis. Burton adds, "I think prayer is critical but I also think that it's important not to rely on prayer only in times of need. That tends to be the habit. But if we are in constant connection with God when things are going great then you open up the spiritual connection that gives you the strength to get through really difficult times."

Study God's word. Bible study provided me with a clearer understanding of what God's purpose was for my life. That's something I had to learn the hard way because I really wasn't an advocate of reading the Bible. I didn't understand it, and that certainly didn't make me want to study it. As far as I was concerned, it was old-time. Why should I care what folks did in the past? But tragic circumstances helped me understand the Bible's relevance as well as its application. I not only wanted to read God's word, I felt compelled to do it. I've read so much of the Bible at this point that I know now why God allowed it to be written. It's to help us get through life's trials and tribulations. If you'll notice, there isn't a tragedy on earth that we are going through today that wasn't discussed in the Bible. It touches on famine, anger, divorce, death, emotional scars, fear, unforgiveness, unemployment, disease, sickness, challenges of the spirit, deceit, and anything else you can think of. It's all in there. But beyond just illustrating the circumstances, God also provides direction on how to get through those challenges by relying on his love and mercy. Today, I read the Bible daily as proof that I will always be blessed through my challenges as long as I continue to trust God. The Bible taught me a new way of life and since I've discovered everything it has to offer I continue to read it regularly and rely on it for guidance.

NEHEMIAH 1:4
When I heard these things, I sat down and wept. For some days I mourned and fasted and prayed before the God of heaven.

HAVE FAITH

Now prayer isn't a one-time thing. You'll need to P.U.S.H. at various stages of your development and in different points in life. This chapter closes by asking you to look at your current circumstance as an opportunity for you to become more spiritual and invites you to make a list of all of the things you can do to develop a better relationship with your creator. With prayer, faith and patience, we'll get through this—I promise.

Find a church or place of worship that suits you. After going from church to church, following my diagnosis of breast cancer and trying to find myself, I went to storefront churches. I went to hallelujiah healing services. I went to Lutheran churches and Catholic churches. I went to the first Baptist, the second Baptist, and the Tabernacle. I even went to a church called the "Whosoever Will Church of God and Christ," and it wasn't until I found a church at which I felt at home that I knew that I could be taught the word of God.

Still as I went to these various houses of worship, I had an opportunity to see other sisters who were enjoying the different churches and everything they had to offer, including the services, people, music, and fellowship. I realized that choosing a church is not so much about what the church is doing but what you personally need in order to grow. During my childhood, I always went to the church that was *chosen for me* by my mother, grandmother, and even my dad. It wasn't until I was hit with tragedy that I realized that I needed to find a place of worship that would help me be more spiritually connected to God and his purpose for my life. I also remember, when I was visiting these different churches, that each one of them had something beautiful to offer. When I went to the healing service, not only did I get a chance to scream, holler, and let loose some of my most angry and frustrated feelings, it really helped me to heal. When I went to churches that were very quiet (Methodist churches are generally quiet), I had a chance to be quiet and hear God's word. Visiting a diverse selection of churches helped me to decide where I wanted to go on a regular basis.

Church is where I got a lot of my personal healing and strength. In addition, church is where I was able to meet other sisters that were just like me with their own crosses to bear. I ended up going to Brooklyn Tabernacle, a church that provided both healing and teaching. The distance from Yonkers, New York, to Brooklyn Tabernacle was very taxing but that's really where I needed to go at that time when I was surviving breast cancer. Now that I am married, with a son, I chose a church closer to home so that we could attend services on a more regular basis and be a part of their weekly programs. Currently, I am a member of Greater Centennial African Methodist Episcopal Church.

So, my sister, I ask you to find yourself a place of worship. It will ensure that you heal your broken heart because it will be filled with the presence of God, and you'll learn how to have a personal relationship with him. Now I know that there are a lot of churches that are not speaking to the needs of women, families, and communities but remember that people and churches are imperfect and that there is only one true perfect being and that's God. So you may have to search high and low to find a church that's right for you. But it's worth the effort. So be determined.

Surround yourself with people that will support your healing. Trust me there are a lot of women and men that don't believe in God or church. Some people will even try to convince you to go to therapy, insisting that a good therapist is all you need. I tried going to a therapist. In fact, I tried two therapists, and what I realized is that these therapists spoke nothing about faith. When I questioned them about their faith, they had no response. And since I have always been a part of a family that has always believed that there is something greater then ourselves in existence, I needed to counsel with people that had the same mindset. I have always had faith, which is the evidence of things hoped for but not seen. I had to realize that people did not have to believe in God if they didn't want to, but I surely knew that believing in God was the only way that I was going to pull out of my tragedy. So I had to surround myself with people that had that same motivation, and those who didn't believe I had to love from a distance.

I remember when I went to the type of church that offered healing services, where we hollered, screamed, prayed, and I asked God to help me with several things in my life. I asked for everything from God's forgiveness to asking Him to look after my family and asking God to help me heal and live. Then I remember telling a friend of mine about that type of service I'd attended. She couldn't understand why I attended that type of church because she didn't think those churches accomplished anything in the community. In her opinion, "brothers are still on the corner even though those churches are doing that type of preaching, so what's the point?" First, we debated back and forth on the issue. But then I decided that I needed the church with the hollering and screaming because I believed it was going to help me heal. I stopped debating with her about where I wanted to go on my spiritual walk and never discussed my faith with her again. I didn't want her to plant a bad seed in my walk with God. Instead, I decided that she had to walk in my shoes to understand the type of healing that I needed. The same thing may apply to you.

You may find that the friends or family that have been around you all of your life don't support your new walk with God or your personal healing. Just remember that you only live once and if you allow someone else to tell you how to heal it could cost you your life.

Make improvements in your home church (whether that's in your heart, your residence, or house of worship). When I joined Brooklyn Tabernacle, I went for worship service in the morning and then I left, and that's how it was every Sunday for me. But during the other six days out of the week, I needed something that would keep me charged. Since my home church was so physically far away, I chose to have prayer groups at home. This made my home a sweeter place.

There is something about the sweetness of prayer that stays within a home when several people get together and pray. After that I realized that church is not just within the four walls of a steepled church but was wherever I went. My real first church was my home and my second church was the place where I worshipped on Sunday mornings. As I started making changes in my home, I got rid of the ritualistic African statues on my walls in my home. Even though they exemplified my Afrocentricity, they were very scary looking statues and I really didn't like looking at them. They almost reminded me of how hard we as people of color have had it in this country and in our homeland. I also colorized my walls, painting over the dull white walls that were throughout my apartment. I painted them green and mauve. Then I added live flowers. And when Christmas rolled around (which was the first official holiday without my husband), I got the biggest tree ever. My home became my sanctuary.

Improve your quality of life. I urge you to decide what changes you need to make to help you improve your quality of life. Sit back and investigate the things that keep you from being connected spiritually. Once you change those things, I can't promise you a perfect life but I can definitely promise that you'll be on your way toward forging ahead on your new spiritual walk.

When I made a commitment to heal, I completely revamped my life. I decided to change my home, join a church, select the type of people that would continue to nurture my spirit, and attend spiritual retreats. I also became more conscious of the things I wore as well as the things I said. I ditched the foul language and stopped hanging out at parties and nightclubs. I also stopped listening to music that made me feel bad about myself as a woman and started inviting more positive sisters to visit me at home. Moreover, I stopped listening to negative news. The results: pure positivity in every area of my life. And this created an environment where God could do his best work.

Enhance your surroundings. I know we've talked about improving your home church, which could be where you live, but I also did certain small things to enhance my surroundings. For example, as soon as I had a little money to play with I purchased a beautiful bed set and very sweet scented candles. Then, I installed light dimmers in every room to add warmth and set a pleasant mood. I also changed the way I purchased food by buying organic foods and buying raw fruits and vegetables in hopes they would keep me alive. Redesigning my environment inspired me to keep fruit in my home. So I filled bowls in my bedroom and kitchen with grapes and oranges.

What was the point? Changing my surroundings helped me to put away the bad memories so I could embrace my future. I encourage you to do the same.

Develop a winning attitude. I would love to say that I developed my own winning attitude, but it was on the backs of those who believed in me and encouraged me to believe that I could win. They gave me the ability to acquire a more positive outlook. Outside of my home and church, I still had to face doctors, bosses, or other negative forces. But if not for doctors who believed that I could live, employers who sent flowers to my home, coworkers who constantly took me out to lunch, and neighbors who made dinner for me while I was going through chemotherapy, I may not have believed that I could be a winner. Once I decided to share my problems with others, they helped me develop a winning attitude. Don't hide your tragedy. You never know who will help you win.

Choose happiness over despair. Over and over again, I had to continue to tell myself that I am happy. There were many times—when I lost a child, had a section of my right breast removed, or lost my second child—that I could have chosen not to be happy. Had I chosen despair, I would have pointed to my issues of fear and pain as the culprits that stole my personal happiness. But what would have been the point? Playing the blame game wouldn't have helped anything. Instead, every morning when I wake up, I choose happiness. It could be because I have a fear of losing my joy. Or, maybe it's because I simply believe that I truly deserve to be happy. In any case, I realize that being happy is a choice. Will you choose happiness over despair?

Listen to God's voice for guidance. I remember when I was a child and the elders of the church would always say that they heard God's voice. I never believed them until I was thirty-four years old and heard it myself. For me, the voice of God responded right after I had a conversation with one of my friends. I was trying to convince her not to be so controlling and I asked her to stay with her husband. By the end of our chat, the young lady decided to go back to her husband that night. When I was alone, praying for her, I heard God speaking to me, asking that I take control of my life. It was the sweetest voice I'd ever heard. He was practically begging me to give him my life, and he told me that if I did he would grant me the desires of my heart. When I retell the story, some people believe and others give me an unconvinced look. But if I kept that experience to myself, then someone else might not have the benefit of my testimony. Today, I've never heard God's voice as clearly as I did that day. But when I think of the good of others and myself, I do hear him.

When do you hear God's voice? If you haven't heard his voice by now, maybe it's because you're not listening. Be quiet and pay attention to the good that God is trying to share with you. Maybe you won't have the same experience that I did. But you *can* communicate with him through prayer. I can't tell you when you should pray, how long you should pray, or what you should even pray about. But I can tell you to pray until something happens (P.U.S.H.) and something will happen—you just wait and see.

STRENGTHEN YOUR FAITH

Linnie Frank and Andria Hall, authors of *This Far By Faith: How to Put God First in Everyday Living*, offer two ways to "start speaking faith today, and watch your actions and belief follow":

EVEN IF YOU HAVE DOUBTS, DON'T EXPRESS THEM. *If you're not quite sure you will receive a healing or a blessing, be able to pay a bill or find a job, by no means voice your fears. Instead, affirm that you will, rather than you won't. Don't look for proof; remember Hebrews 11:1 (King James Version): "Faith is the substance of things hoped for, the evidence of things not seen."*

TRAIN YOURSELF. *Begin by speaking what it is you want to believe, then the Father in Heaven will reward you with increased faith. Don't speak words of untruth, words of sickness, despair, hopelessness, and defeat. If you need fortifying, go to the Bible. You will find example after example of how we've already been delivered through the promises of God. Find scriptures to stand on, and then when you're feeling heavy-laden, use the Word as your comfort and guide. That's why they call it the Living Bible!*

Step 2

Rally Up Support

Sisters who gathered with me two
months after my diagnosis

1/15/96
Terrie keeps sending me all of these articles on cancer survivors. Initially, I couldn't understand why she was sending me these things. After all, I didn't care about anyone else dying of cancer. I really wasn't interested in hearing their cancer stories.

But now I finally see her point. If those people are fighting, I can too. I can beat this.

Those articles feature young women, old women, and people of all races. They're still living and enjoying their lives.

Terrie has shown me the meaning of true love and so have so many other people that I've met along the way.

There was no reason for them to care about me. They didn't know me that well and we weren't even great friends. But since my diagnosis people have been going out of their way to care for me and I can't understand why.

One of my friends keeps offering to come over to help out. She says she'll cook, shop, wash clothes, or anything else that I need her to do. She even says she'll work in silence just so she wouldn't bother me. Her offer and the offers from others have been amazing and their kindness is well beyond anything I could have ever expected.

For a long time, I wondered why God would allow this to happen to me. I just kept thinking, why me? But now I'm thinking, why not me?

If God hadn't given me cancer, look at all of the love I would have missed.

When I was deep into my own drama, I needed a sistah to just sit down and kick it with. I'm talking about a real sistah, one that wouldn't judge me because I didn't curb my language or put up a front to pretend my life was without a spot or wrinkle. We could talk about everything from child molestation to the last boyfriend we were intimate with and, more importantly, the mistakes we made. We could talk about the last time we got fired from a job and cry in each other's arms about family issues. We kept it real.

You need people that allow you to keep it real. You need to surround yourself with good friends that you feel safe and comfortable with. You need some folks that will allow you to be vulnerable and won't hold it against you. You need people that have your back.

Now, I know it's hard to ask other people for help and support. If you're anything like me, you're used to handling your business all by yourself. You take pride in the fact that you don't rely on anyone but yourself for results and you probably feel very secure in that approach. Well, I've got news for you. As much as you thought you were doing things on your own, you really weren't. You just failed to acknowledge the people and the sources that assisted you. I guarantee you that tragedy will help you have a greater appreciation for the people that lend their support, now you just have to work on showing your gratitude to those who deserve it. In addition, tragedy will force you not only to accept help from others but actually ask for assistance in your time of need. Your self-proclaimed "superwoman" armor is one of the first of many defenses you'll need to shed if you're ever going to come out on top. The sooner you face that reality, the sooner you'll get on the path to healing.

The benefits to having a strong support team in place are both mental and physical. From a psychological standpoint, "a good social support system can help reduce stress," according to realage.com, a Web site designed to provide surfers with tips on how they can develop a healthier lifestyle. The site goes on to say that "having friends or family upon whom you can rely during tough times is a great stress management tool." And the reduced stress helps to strengthen the immune system, that's the body's protective mechanism for fighting diseases and other disorders. So start putting together a strong support team as soon as the need arises because your physical and mental health could depend on it.

I never thought that I would be dependent on other people because I was convinced that I really could do it all—without anyone else's help. What a joke. With the death of a child, an ectopic pregnancy, and breast cancer, I realized just how much I needed other people. And I also found out just how much they needed me too. Contrary to what you might believe, your tragic experience is not just about *you*. If you think that, you couldn't be more wrong. People learn by experiencing as well as by witnessing the experiences of others. So when we go through things, our responses teach the people around us how to do the right thing or how to do the wrong thing. I bet you didn't know that God was using you and your circumstance so that you can educate others. But that's exactly what you're doing.

Through tragedy, life's perils and promises are revealed and they teach God's children to be grateful, mindful, fearful, and resilient. In addition, the way others react to your situation helps them discover things about themselves that may not otherwise have been revealed to them. With that said, know that when you deny people the opportunity to help you, you are preventing them from learning something that God has specifically designed for them to acquire through your experience.

LEVITICUS 25:35
If one of your countrymen becomes poor and is unable to support himself among you, help him as you would an alien or a temporary resident, so he can continue to live among you.

Take my friend Terry Chapman, for example. She lost a dear friend of hers one year before I told her that I had cancer. At the time, she was grieving over her friend, a thirty-two-year-old wife who worked as an underwriter for a life insurance company. Although this young woman started out at the company as a lower-level clerk, she had received several promotions and was still moving up at the job. "Mary (not her real name) and I worked together for eight years," Terry told me. "Our relationship became more than just coworkers, and I was devastated when she was diagnosed with breast cancer."

According to Terry, Mary was in denial during her bout with breast cancer and she refused get the proper treatment in time due to this denial. Also, she was unable to give up many of the foods and bad habits—like smoking—that the doctors suggested. As a result, her time on earth after she was diagnosed with breast cancer was short. "The cancer had spread to her brain and within days she was put in a hospice. Mary was in such denial that in the beginning she was even trying to get pregnant. Before I knew it, she had died," Terry reminisces. "When you called a year later, crying over the phone telling me that you had breast cancer, I said to God, 'Please don't take another friend.'"

Terry asked God to use her and show her how she could help me. She recognized the same behavior in me that she did in her friend. I also started off in shock and denial. And since those were signs Terry had seen before, she feared I'd take the same path as Mary. But instead of giving way to her fears, Terry used her experience and the knowledge that she'd gained from working as a medical underwriter at a major insurance carrier to help me understand the options that were available to me. She was well-versed in medical jargon and used that skill to keep me informed.

"That's what friends are for," Terry insists. She says in times of duress you should be able to lean on your friends. "My main focus was to try to be a place of support to help you talk about your feelings. You were in shock and angry. Now sometimes that anger was displaced and directed at me, but I was okay with that because I understood the process."

Terry was also in a place where she was having a major spiritual awakening. The Holy Spirit would speak to her, and she'd write things down to capture His message. "And one thing that came up was a letter that he wanted me to give you. But I didn't know how you'd react because at one point you had thrown one of those information packets back in my face. You were in a place of fear and wanted to stay there licking your wounds. So when the Holy Spirit gave me this letter, I didn't know if you were going to attack me for being too pushy. I didn't know what was going to happen, but I felt I had to do this. I prayed, fasted, and asked God to do whatever he needed to do to use me, and I was willing to accept the consequences. I realized the situation was bigger than me, bigger than our friendship, and your life was at stake."

Terry believed that her divinely inspired letter was going to make a huge impact, and it did. She read the letter to me and told me things about my life that I'd never shared with anyone. As she recited it, I just sat there shaking the entire time. I started to cry but Terry just kept rubbing my back and holding my hand until she finished reading. At the conclusion, we embraced and my emotional gates opened up so I could release all of the pain. I was touched in a way that I can't describe. The letter contained things in it that I'd never told Terry, so I guess God told her those things to help her prove that the letter was indeed authentic. It also talked about faith and assured me that I could do all things through Christ that strengthens me, but it also told me that I needed to act so that my faith could be released. It promised that God would not forsake me. That letter helped me make the decision to move forward with my cancer treatment despite my fears. Prior to that, I was at a standstill. I truly believe that Terry was my personal messenger from God. But I may never have enjoyed that benefit if I hadn't allowed her to support me and help me take the step that I needed to save my life.

But what did helping me do for Terry? "I was honored that God would use me in that way and that Mary's death was not in vain," she says. For a while, Terry still found it hard to come to terms with her friend's death. "I kept asking God why Shellie and not Mary. But God told me not to question it. It was a release for Mary to die because she was going through so much. But God had a great work for you. Shellie, we didn't realize how big this was going to be. It amazes me how God has used you to help so many other women. Now, I'm at peace."

So if I'd prevented Terry from helping me then, I would have also blocked the blessing that God had for her. I would have been a barrier between her and one of life's lessons that was designed specifically for her benefit. Aside from that, I learned a lot about myself, both as a cancer survivor and a human being, by interfacing with other people. I think the world is designed that way.

2 SAMUEL 22:19
They confronted me in the day of my disaster, but the LORD was my support.

The lessons came in various forms. Sometimes they were in bits and pieces. Other times they were truly bricks that hit me over the head. Through my education, I followed my heart for understanding and that led me down a journey of enlightenment that reinforced just how much I needed other people in my life.

My family and friends have been a critical force in my healing, even though I didn't appreciate them at first. As I said, Terry helped me get over the initial shock of my diagnosis but different people stepped in to support me in other ways. My mother, for instance, was with me when I woke up from the hospital after I had the lumpectomy. My mom also helped me search for a second opinion, and even provided me with the comic relief that I needed. And then there was the assistance that came from my husband's cousin, who lived downstairs from me. He was a practicing physician at Albert Einstein and he'd often offer to give me a lift to my chemotherapy treatments. My husband's family also called to check on me from time to time. So even though my husband was acting like a complete jerk, his family was gracious and gave me the support I needed.

Others—people who didn't even know me—stepped up to the plate as well. All their efforts inspired me to keep living and loving every moment of the life that I had left. It also made me wonder where I would have been if I didn't have them. We all need somebody to lean on, so don't be afraid to reach out and touch someone. And don't be surprised when they reach back.

There are all types of links that you can make to assist in your healing. Some connections may be informal, including friends, family members and coworkers. Other connections you'll need are formal, including support groups, social workers, health experts, Web sites, magazines, media groups, and professional associations. In this chapter, we'll explore how and when you should tap either of the two networks. More importantly, this chapter will show you how to fight—not as a boxer but as a survivor. This mode requires that you surround yourself with people that are going to motivate you to overcome a challenge even when you're ready to give up. When you're facing adversity, the last thing you need is a pity party. What you need is a power party. So let's get ready to rumble.

PSALMS 20:2
May he send you help from the sanctuary and grant you support from Zion.

YOUR POWER PARTY

If you're ready to enter fight mode (and this should be done as soon as possible), start planning your "power" party where crying and sad songs are strictly forbidden. Your mission is to develop a recovery strategy so you can ensure a more fulfilling life. Now here you can take the word "party" in the literal sense and actually get your support team together to strategize, or you can just have a "party" in your mind at which you think of all the people you need to help you deal with this latest life challenge. Perhaps you'll do both. The point here is to start enlisting positive people to support you as you fight one of the biggest battles of your life.

"Having a support system is crucial," according to my godmother, Marie Williams, whose background is in social work. "Support is one of the most important aspects to survival. Your support system doesn't always have to be your family members. As far as I'm concerned, whoever is there for you gets to be your family. The word family doesn't always have to mean blood relatives. Every person, whether they recognize it or not, needs a support system. It's the key to survival in a time of need. I think people shouldn't be afraid to reach out to one another. Sometimes it's hard to find someone to trust, I can understand that. I have a close friend who told me that if it wasn't for me, she wouldn't be around today. It took a lot for me to break through her mistrust. I let her know that I was extending my hand to help her but it was up to her to take the support. She took the risk. And that's how your support system can start to form. You have to take some risks and believe that people genuinely mean it when they say they are here for you. You'll know when something isn't right. There is that instinct, or gut feeling, that will kick in. If you pray and meditate spiritually, you'll get that gut feeling when things aren't quite right and you can trust that. But at the same time, you have to be willing to give someone a chance to help you if you truly want to heal."

Marie is actually my "adopted" godmother. After I saw how much she cared for me and realized how much of a blessing she was in my life, I asked her if she would be my godmother and she said, "Yes." Like she says, family doesn't necessarily mean blood relatives and she helped me realize that. But I would have never been able to experience her love unless I trusted her and allowed her to help me heal. I encourage you to do the same. Consider adopting someone into your life for support. Remember, it's never too late to have a happy childhood, and there is no time like the present to get the support you need.

So, how can you get others to help you overcome this challenge? Well first you have to open your door and let them share your experience. When you allow them to help you, trust me, God will bless you. And get in the habit of saying yes. A lot of times we miss out on what we need because we're afraid of asking for what we want or we don't feel comfortable accepting what other people offer us. Girlfriend, it's okay to admit that you can't do it all. And even if you can do some things, there are times when others are more equipped, more qualified, or simply just in a better position than we are. It's okay. It doesn't mean that there's anything wrong with you, it just means that you're human. And sometimes God forces us to need others so we can appreciate life's blessings as well as gain a clearer understanding of the forces that are at work in our lives. It's all a part of the plan.

That was a hard lesson for Julia Boyd, clinical psychotherapist and author of *In the Company of My Sisters*. "When I was in graduate school, my friend would say 'Let me make dinner for you and your son.' And I'd offer to get the groceries until they convinced me that when they offered to make dinner, that meant everything was included," she explains. "See, I was always concerned with how I was going to pay them back. But one friend set me straight by telling that all she wanted to know was that when she needed me, I'd be there for her in whatever form—for her that was enough. Recently, I had surgery and the doctor told me that I couldn't lift anything heavier than a notebook for the next two to three months. So when I had to go grocery shopping, my friend offered to take me, reminding me that I couldn't lift anything. I needed that friend to remind me that it was okay for me not to do everything myself."

ROMANS 11:18
Do not boast over those branches. If you do, consider this: You do not support the root, but the root supports you.

According to Boyd, sometimes we don't even know what support looks like. But now she's not only learning what help looks like, she's defining it based on what she needs. "Whenever I go on tour, I have three friends that, no matter where I am, no matter what time of day it is, I can call," she states proudly. "They know when they hear my voice that I need to talk," and sometimes it's that type of comfort that helps her move forward. Now Boyd has no trouble having someone make her bed or even walk her dog because she's given herself permission to take care of herself and knows at times that means relying on other people. "I've got a lot of what I know about being self sufficient from my mother, who was big on doing for yourself," she admits.

But now she doesn't see asking for help as a weakness. "We [black women] are fearful of others judging us, and that fear gets in the way. If you viewed me as weak, then I felt I didn't measure up. But now I know it's not about measuring up, it's about taking care of me."

So take good care of yourself. If someone offers to help you with the kids, let them. If someone offers to do your laundry, let them. If someone offers to rub your feet (and you don't run the risk of ruining a committed relationship, of course), let them. Allowing people to care for you and love you is one way that you can honor yourself, and that's important in the healing process.

Now what if there are things that you need that haven't been offered to you? Ask for them. When I need something, I call and ask. Now, because I care about people, I am careful about whom I ask and what I ask them to do. Not everyone has the means and the time to assist, but I choose carefully those I know can be strong enough and capable enough to assist me. For example, if your sister has five kids at home, a husband, and her own family drama, don't ask her to do something that is almost impossible for her to complete. Choose wisely. In addition, ask people who you know you get along with and who will do things for you cheerfully. You don't want to deal with someone who will depress you and make you feel worse than before. But the point here is to ask for what you need. As the Bible says, you have not because you ask not. So find people in your circle that can support you as you muddle through whatever situation you're experiencing.

On another note, ask for things that you really need so that the people around you don't feel exploited. Try making a list of all the things you need to get through the next few days. Your list should include everything from doing the laundry to making funeral arrangements and think of people who can support you in those tasks. It's time to delegate. Keep in mind, however, that "support" may or may not mean "doing" certain tasks. Perhaps support can come in the form of accompanying you to the doctor's visit and holding your hand. Or, maybe you can handle doing your own laundry but you just need someone to sit with you while you wait for your clothes to dry. Be specific in your requests and only involve people that you trust. And give yourself permission to lean on others for support and guidance, knowing that things can *still* move in the right direction even if you're not in the driver's seat.

THE GUEST LIST

In 1999, I spoke at North General Hospital about surviving cancer. Then in 2001, I was driving by North General and something told me to call and ask if they had an ongoing support group. I figured that I could teach aerobics on-site. Well, when I called I spoke with D. G. Wilson Davis, who was hosting a survivor group called FORCE (Focus on Rehabilitation and Cancer Education). I then told her that I would love to come and teach fitness for a day to her survivors and she was elated. Upon meeting her, I realized that she was definitely someone I wanted on my support team and D. G. and I have been fighting for survivors ever since. D. G. was not only living with cancer, she was telling all cancer survivors that we would live, too. According to D. G., having cancer only meant we had to take an unexpected step along life's course but that still didn't mean we should quit. I fell in love with her spirit. She is calm, cool, and apprehensive. I am excited, energetic, and assertive. We are a great team. But D. G., is just one of the people on my support team, here are others:

Jeff Berman: A cancer survivor who currently heads FORCE on a full-time basis and is the author of *The Force Program: The Proven Way to Fight Cancer Through Movement and Exercise*. He established an exercise support program for people with cancer, which FORCE adopted five years later. For the past two years, I have been helping lead his group at the Harlem YMCA. His program has helped the women of Harlem to stay focused on surviving cancer as well as to educate them on a new healthy lifestyle. We met through D. G. Wilson Davis and are very good friends. In fact, the three of us are inseparable.

Brenda Anderson: My mom is extremely cautious. But what do you expect? I'm her only daughter. Nevertheless, she was another driving force that helped me to consider chemo as a treatment option, and she was always there with this sense of urgency. I needed that because sometimes I tend to procrastinate out of fear. My mom had enough fear for the both of us but she still pushed for action.

Terrie Williams: Terrie assured me that I had a home away from home by connecting me with some powerful women in her own family. She also sent me every article under the sun about what other cancer survivors were doing across the globe—proving that there is life after cancer. These women were courageous while facing adversity that was far more challenging than I was experiencing. Yet, they were achieving their dreams. That was powerful. Aside from transforming me into a cancer specialist, Terrie also helped me feel empowered.

Terry Chapman: Girlfriend went with me to my first chemotherapy treatment and stuck with me on the doctor visits that followed. Now that's support. She would ask all the relevant questions, even when I didn't have a clue about what was happening to me or when I didn't have the courage to find out. She felt that she could be objective enough to get the facts so that she and I could further discuss them when I was ready. After each doctor session, she would then break everything down in laymen terms so I could understand what the doctor was saying about me. Nobody should face such a challenge alone so make sure you have a Terry to help support you.

Jennifer Jones: Now we were close girlfriends before I got sick but the illness drew us closer to each other. Jennifer took our relationship to a new level when she realized there was a possibility that she could lose me. She wanted me to live and showed me that belief whenever she could during her frequent visits from Washington, D.C. Her unconditional love was so overwhelming because there were so many people who didn't have time or couldn't be there for me. God gave me Jennifer as a sign that I would be missed.

Marie Williams: My godmother is my rock. She checked on me daily and made it clear that I could call her morning, noon, and night. As a social worker, she has the education and probably the natural ability to help in trying times but our relationship developed a degree of intimacy that went way beyond her call of duty. She gave her personal time to counsel me, to rise above my disease and to help me change my way of thinking. After my husband abandoned me, she was the first person I called.

Robert Anderson: My dad and his church prayed for me constantly and my dad sent me some prayer clothes to put on my breasts. My dad was also a special source of inspiration. As someone who has survived kidney failure for over thirty years, my dad made me realize that I came from quality stock. His faith in God and in me helped me to have faith in my recovery.

Cheryl and Jimmy Lewis: Now these two became my New York–based sister and brother. When I didn't want to be alone in Westchester, I could always go to Cheryl and Jimmy's house in Harlem at any time during the day or night. For example, one time after midnight I just couldn't sleep, I don't know if it was out of fear, loneliness, or both. Anyway, I tapped on Cheryl and Jimmy's door and they opened it with open arms. "We've been waiting for you," they'd say. And I knew I was home.

In selecting the people you want on your support team, choose carefully. People say and do some angry, vicious things to one another. They can be mean, selfish, and afraid. And as far as I'm concerned, those are issues that *they* have to deal with on their own time. I assess my relationships on a regular basis by looking at where I want to go in my life. If the person and myself seem to be headed in the same direction, I keep them around. If not, I either move on or change our level of intimacy. Otherwise, I'd just be an obstacle preventing them from doing what they need to do, or the reverse.

According to Debrena Jackson Gandy, author of *All the Joy You Can Stand,* when you're going through times it's important to have people in your life that can speak to your spirit. "When you're in a tragedy, your energy is so consumed by the situation that the level of emotional, spiritual, and psychic energy you need to expend goes way up, it takes a big leap," she explains. "So when people can speak into your spirit, they can give you the strength you need to keep going by helping you shed light and give meaning to the situation. This becomes so critical because you can have a nervous breakdown if you don't have your spirit refueled and the right support."

Another way to reshape your relationships is to reevaluate how you spend your time and where you spend it. People with common interests are drawn to the same things. Thus, if you are a drinker, the people that are drawn to you will most likely hang out in bars. If you are an athlete, associates will be active in sports or at the very least sports fans. By the same token, if you spend most of your free time at church gatherings, you'll be surrounded by church members—just request that they pray for you and the resolution of your circumstance.

I changed my life and circle of friends by doing things that changed my spirit. Although I've always had good friends, I needed

A WORD ABOUT FAITH

When choosing a support team remember to choose people who have faith. There have been lots of times when I have sought counsel from therapists, friends, family, and neighbors. Though they had the best advice in the world they didn't have faith and only served to diminish my dreams. There are people who only believe in what they see. Trust me, had I lived my life only by what I could see I would be dead by now. Faith surpasses all understanding. And it was faith that sustained my emotional and physical health.

more. I needed to be around sisters who shared my vision. My sentence with cancer was so painful that at times I didn't think I'd make it. As a result, it was essential to be with a crowd that could help me believe I could survive: If I had surrounded myself with the dying, I'm sure I wouldn't have been around to write this book. I encourage you to do the same: Immerse yourself among people that have a zest for life so you can catch their enthusiasm and strengthen your faith.

PARTY TALK

We keep hammering away that if you want something, you need to just ask for it. But, maybe you're not asking because you don't know how. There are ways to ask for things that you want so that people that you're speaking to know where you're coming from and can respond freely about their ability to help you. In Terrie Williams's book *The Personal Touch,* she talks about how being open and honest with people can help you connect with them on a personal, human level. "And if you can be blunt, open and honest," she writes, "more often than not it makes everyone feel more comfortable." She is specifically suggesting this approach for use in a business setting, but I think this approach could work in our personal lives as well.

Debrena Jackson Gandy, author of *All the Joy You Can Stand: 101 Sacred Power Principles for Making Joy Real in Your Life,* agrees that it's important to communicate what's happening to you with the people with whom you interact. Some people just drop out of sight when things go awry, and then they have to start an intense cleanup job to get things back on track when they're ready to come back to earth. Bad idea. According to Gandy, a tragedy is not the time to go into isolation mode:

When I was in the thick of things with my marriage, folks were calling me, e-mailing me and sending me cards, but I also called people to tell them what was going on. I wasn't trying to do business as usual. I would call someone to say that I was feeling weak that day. I'd ask someone to pray for me or pray with me. There was always someone to speak into my spirit but I was always proactive. I did what I needed to do so I wouldn't sink into an abyss.

I suggest that others do the same. You can be more formal and ask people to come over to pray for you. A lot of times if we make a request and let it be known, people will show up. Don't assume they won't until you give them a chance. I hear people complain about not getting support until I ask them, "Do people know what you are going through?" A lot of people don't know you need their support. But if you're able to let people know how they can best support you, they can be extremely helpful.

The things that people said to me when I went through my own trying time were very supportive. Some prayed for me or shared powerful words. Sometimes what they said became my word for the day. I realized that I wasn't alone. People ended up sharing intimate stuff with me because I was just real and didn't try to cover things up. I didn't necessarily give details but I gave information that was appropriate for the relationship. It gave people compassion. They understood that I didn't have the psychic and emotional energy to attend business functions and they allowed me to reschedule. Many of those people I've since reconnected with when things got back on track. The support was amazing and it lightened my load.

Make specific requests. Reach out and allow people to help you. Tell the truth about where you are and what space you're in. People love to help when they know what form it needs to come in. Don't just wait for the help, seek it out and create it. People feel very liberated in sharing and supporting you. Beyond that, they love to deliver when they know exactly what they should do for you.

Well said, sis. I first tested this approach on my job. I was really scared about going to work after being diagnosed with cancer. I was convinced that everyone would treat me differently or just wouldn't understand what I was going through. Anyway, I went in to my job at the Society of Motion Pictures and Television Engineers and was pleasantly surprised. When I told my boss what the deal was, people were very understanding. There were times when I had to leave early because I was sick and my boss, John Izzo, told me I could go anytime. He was really good with handling my situation. Now when I lost all of my hair that was a challenge. I started getting really angry on the job and everything bothered me. I remember snapping at my boss for really no reason and I realized I had to get a grip on myself. Still, my boss was understanding of my situation. I also confided in two of my coworkers who really prayed with me constantly and were always there to listen me. They made the workday easier to deal with because they shared my pain. Being able to continue to work was a real blessing for me. I had just decided that if I was going to live that I was going to have to work. And if I was going to stay on the job, that meant telling people that I was going through a challenge. And that was that.

PSALMS 119:105
Your word is a lamp to my feet and a light for my path.

I also learned to communicate better with my family. Whenever I would share a life experience with my aunt she would always tell me to say what I mean. "Don't hold back. Be honest, persuasive, and tell people what you need," she'd say firmly. Her feeling was that I needed to be honest and not to pretend that everything was okay when it was not. "People need to know when it's okay for them to call or visit you. Otherwise, you are going to make enemies, because when you don't tell people the truth they may say and do things that may make you very angry and have no idea what ticked you off."

She was right about that. For instance, when I lost my first child my cousin would call me often to see how I was doing. But then she'd start crying on the phone because my situation was upsetting to her. For two weeks, I found myself trying to console her until I finally set some boundaries. I told her that I was really going through a lot and I found her calls depressing. "I'll call you if something changes," I said, ending the conversation. She wanted me to reassure her that everything was going to be okay, but at that point, I needed to be concerned about what I was dealing with at the time. As Terrie suggested, sometimes it takes being direct.

I also learned to ask for small things. There have been several times when I just needed company. So I asked my godmother to take me on walks with her. That really made me feel good. Then I told my friend Jennifer that I needed to visit Washington, D.C. and see all the different places I remembered from my childhood. She volunteered to be my tour guide and we visited four different locations, which included all three elementary schools I attended and every apartment complex we lived in. It was very emotional, too, because when I went back I would relive my happy and sad times as a child. We ended our visit with prayer and I thanked Jennifer for being so patient.

These experiences helped me realize just how much I needed other people. Then when people called to ask what I needed, I would tell them. It took the focus off of my pride and shined the spotlight on my ultimate goal: healing. So I'd ask if people could pick me up a few groceries when they went out or loan me a Kirk Franklin CD. Sometimes I'd invite people to just watch a movie with me or play a round of cards. Or sometimes I'd invite people to come over for a word of prayer. Needing people enabled me to let God do His best work.

Sis, it's okay to need people. Man (or woman) was not meant to walk this earth alone. Sometimes, I think we go through things just so we are forced to reconnect with society. So let your challenge provide you with a license to call on the troops. People genuinely want to help you get over that hump you're now facing, you just need to allow them to do it.

Many times we don't want to call on people because we don't want them to call on us for anything. We fear that we'll owe somebody something. But you should want to be there for somebody else because that's the only reason we're all on the planet—to support one another. God ensures that a selfish person is a lonely person. Trust me, I know. But then I realized the powerful people he put into my life. My friends needed me as much as I needed them.

There's another reason for asking for help, it affirms your self-love. Tonya White, age thirty-seven, tells how her family pulled together when her sister became ill. According to Tonya, the experience helped the family create a stronger bond and forced her to make some important changes in her own life:

My sister's death was the most tragic thing that has happened to me in my life. Her illness came up when I was going through a divorce.

I knew that my marriage was ending in June 1998 and my sister was diagnosed with lymphoma in September 1998. So I was grieving for two different reasons. Because they happened at the same time, I was tested as far as my faith was concerned. But I grew stronger in it because I felt like my continuing to rely on God was the only thing left for me to do. I had no other choice. My faith had always been strong but during that time it got even stronger.

Every morning before I leave for work, I say my prayers and I read daily devotions. First, I started reading daily devotions by Iyanla Vanzant, then I went from that book to another one, My Utmost For His Highest by Oswald Chambers. At one time, I would forget to take time out for devotion because I was in a rush. But during my hard times, I didn't forget. I realized that I had to make the time to read those daily devotions because the text would direct me to different Scriptures that would give me strength and make a difference in my day. So I read the Scripture more and more as well as writing in a journal.

When my family and I first found out about my sister's condition, we were all upset. But she was a fighter and was always positive. Her symptoms started with a cough that just wouldn't go away. It was Labor Day weekend of 1998: She called me and told me that she'd been coughing all night and was going to the emergency room. At first they told her that it was bronchitis. But when she followed up with her primary care physician on that Tuesday, they sent her for X-rays and she called me from the radiologist crying because they told her that they saw a spot on her lungs and wanted to admit her to the hospital for tests. I told her to go home and get her things together while I contacted the family. My mother and her mother, met her at the house and they took her to the hospital. When the results came back on Thursday, they told her that she had cancer of the lymph nodes but they weren't sure how extensive it was. Shortly after, they told us they wanted to start her with

*chemo and radiation. By February, she needed a bone marrow trans-
plant. My younger sister was a 100-percent match so they moved
forward with the surgery. The doctors told us that the cancer was
gone. Everything was positive. We made arrangements for someone
to move in with my sister for support and we took turns staying
with her. She went to the hospital every day for a follow-up and it
seemed that things were looking up.*

*My sister was looking forward to her recovery. She talked
about how even though she was receiving chemo and radiation, she
was still going to try to have a baby if she found the right man. "If
I'm not able to have a baby, I'm going to adopt," she happily concluded. She also talked about traveling and kept a list of places she
was going to try to visit during the year as soon as the doctors gave
her permission to hit the road.*

*Then Memorial Day weekend rolled around. We were at my
mom's house and my sister wanted to go over to her aunt's house
on her mother's side. My mother was concerned because she didn't
think my sister was strong enough to go out yet, but she really
wanted to go, so I took her. The very next day, my mother had to
take her to the hospital. They kept her because of a cough that they
thought was pneumonia. That was on a Monday, by Thursday she
was on a respirator. She was afraid. I had never seen her afraid
through the entire ordeal. The first week she was conscious, the second week she was sedated, and by the third week, you got nothing.
She never got off of the respirator. It seems that the growth that the
doctors thought was gone was actually hidden and, when my sister
caught pneumonia, that continued the damage to her lungs. We
chose not to keep her on the respirator because we didn't have any
other options and she was never going to be able to breathe on her
own. My sister died on June 19, 1999.*

*Writing letters to my sister helps me get through it. When I give
my parents cards, I always sign them from her and me because I*

believe her spirit is alive in all of us. During those hard times, there were lots of prayers and the bond in our family has been strengthened. For example, her mom and I grew even closer during that time. My younger sister and I grew closer. Even though I'm my mother's only child, through her marriage to their father, I got two stepsisters and a stepbrother who have been in my life ever since I was eighteen. We never had any issues and never refer to one another as "step" this or that—we're just family. As far as I was concerned my mother gave birth to them because that's just how close we were. Since my sister's death, we're all even closer because we had to lean on one another.

Seeing what my sister was going through from September to December made me realize how short life really is and that you can't take your time on earth for granted. When a tragedy hit so close to home it forced me to take a look at my own life. I was trying to hold on to the strings of a marriage even though I knew it needed to end. The experience made me realize that I had to make a decision and that decision was to end the marriage. My sister's illness prompted me to move ahead with the divorce because, realistically, my marriage had been over since 1996.

For anyone who's going through something, I recommend that they try to find something that works for them. What worked for me may not necessarily work for them. But they need to continue searching until they find the support they need. Prayer helps as well as continuing to believe that this too shall pass. I know it's a cliché, but it's the truth. I still miss her but I'm not the person that I was in 1999 who was missing her. And my family and I were able to get through the hard times by being there for one another.

What's the first step toward being able to accept help from other people? According to Boyd, you'll be able to accept help from others when you value yourself. She suggests repeating daily affirmations as

47

a way to help us get the support we need. Below are Boyd's favorite affirmations, but feel free to add your own:

- I'm on my way to help.

- I'm the best person I know how to be.

- I'm growing in thought, word, and deed.

- If you want a thing to be, take your time, and go slowly.

- Do one thing and do it well.

- Simple things are holy.

- Slow down, take it one piece at a time.

- We got all the time we need to do whatever it is we need to do.

So how do you make the connection? You can check the Yellow Pages or the Internet for formal support groups or create your own. I remember my friend Cheryl Lane-Lewis having our first girls' day together. She gathered some of her closest friends and all of us first introduced ourselves and then Cheryl gave us all things to discuss. It was great, because that was the beginning of our first sistah club. As our friendship grew, we became more secure with one another and began to share more and more as we grew together. When I got sick they all came over and we hugged and united. I needed them to tell me that I was going to be okay. We prayed and we sang and we cried. They told me the real deal about letting go and letting God, and they told me to not hold on to the pain I was feeling about my ex. My sistahs came through.

Although black women traditionally rely on their sisterhood, community, family, and church for support, know that it's okay to get help from a professional, too. When selecting a therapist, be sure to: (1) determine how you're going to pay for the sessions and select a professional with rates that you can afford over the course of your treatment (if they are not covered by your insurance plan); (2) get referrals from friends, family, or your employer's referral service so you can see someone who is covered under your health plan; (3) research additional tips for selecting a therapist through the Internet or in other publications; (4) be honest with yourself about the type of counselor you think you'd feel comfortable with and seek out that person; and (5) ask lots of questions before and during your session. If you're not happy with the answers, don't be afraid to make a switch. Keep these tips in mind as you get the help you need to recover. For me I need a professional that has faith, a strong belief in something greater than themselves. According to Lori S. Robinson, author of *I Will Survive: The African-American Guide to Healing From Sexual Assault and Abuse*, getting professional support can be essential for a full recovery. Here she shares how therapy helped her heal:

On May 15, 1995, I was raped after coming home from a friend's house one late night after work. I parked my car across the street from my apartment as I normally did. Then I proceeded to gather my belongings. When I got out of the car, I remember that I was a little startled because I saw two men standing on the sidewalk. I hadn't noticed anyone on my block when I first parked. Now there were young black men just hanging around the building as if looking for trouble. Still, I'd convinced myself that there was no reason for me to be afraid. After all, these were brothers, why would they hurt me?

But before I realized it, I was sandwiched by them, even though I hadn't noticed any footsteps. I turned to my right to say hello and the first thing I saw was a gun pointed at my head. The person with the gun yelled at me not to look at him. So I didn't. In fact, I hadn't seen either of their faces. Next, the two of them rushed me up to my apartment. In the hours that followed, I was blindfolded, gagged, tied facedown to my bed, and raped vaginally and anally by both men.

I couldn't hear clearly but after it seemed as if they'd left, I untied myself from the bed. When I went into the living room, I realized they'd stolen all of my electronics. Then, when I managed to make it downstairs, I saw they'd also stolen my car. I scanned the windows in the apartment building until I came across one that looked as though the people inside were still awake. I mustered up the strength I had left to knock on the door. When they answered, I told them—people I'd never seen a day in my life before that moment—that I'd been raped. They called the police and the ambulance. They also allowed me to phone my sister who rushed right over.

Both my sister and the police accompanied me to the hospital, where I was given what's called a rape kit. That's where a gynecologist (another stranger) takes your clothes for further assessment and performs a physical, very intimate, examination to gather evidence and determine your injuries. The process was grueling. I'd just been raped and then I had to have another stranger examine between my legs. It's like an ob-gyn exam. They take samples from your vagina and anus. It's not pleasant—at all. Perhaps my only solace was that the gynecologist was a woman.

How did I feel after being raped? I was more than depressed, more than angry, more than hurt, more than demoralized, and more than distraught. I was totally wiped out and felt horribly violated as I underwent an emotional torture. If I have to categorize it, I would say I was totally devastated. But it truly is a feeling that can't be put into words.

After the ordeal, it was never business as usual. Fortunately, my boss was understanding and told me to take as much time as I needed to recover. I took two weeks off. I never returned to my apartment. My sister and other family members packed all of my belongings for me. I then moved into a townhouse that my sister and I rented from my parents. That one night turned my world upside down, inside out.

Still, I was able to pick up the pieces of my life. I don't want to ever trivialize the healing process and make it sound like it was some easy, quick thing. But I was hopeful that God could help me feel better and heal. I was also very committed to therapy. I had an excellent counselor, who helped me tremendously. My family and friends helped me create a healing environment and people didn't belittle what I'd been through but there was an expectation that I would heal even though we didn't know what that healing would look like.

Sharing helped, too. I wrote about my ordeal in an article for Emerge *magazine*, the publication for which I worked at the time. It seemed very appropriate since there was hoopla surrounding a case about a Spelman College student who'd accused four Morehouse men of rape. I went to Spelman and I was raped, so I could relate. The response to my story was overwhelming and was one of the catalysts that inspired me to write a book to encourage, comfort, and empower other survivors.

As I go from city to city talking to other rape victims, I tell them that healing is possible as long as they reach out for help— particularly from the professionals. I worked very hard at therapy and there are still things about myself I can work to improve and change. A lot of black people have a problem with therapy and counseling but for me that was not an issue. As far as I'm concerned, there are professionals that are trained to help us overcome our challenges. So why not access help? When we have a broken leg or a cold, we don't hesitate to go to a medical doctor. But somehow, we don't practice this when it comes to saving our mental health. As I write in my book, "Being strong and brave is getting help, not suffering in silence."

IMPROVE YOUR MENTAL HEALTH

A Web site, BlackWomensHealth *(www.blackwomenshealth.com)*, designed to provide African-American females with a wealth of health and wellness information offers these suggestions for optimal mental health:

KNOW THYSELF. A healthy identity is critical for overall good mental health. For women of African descent, this means seeing themselves as the recipients of generations of collective wisdom and experience from African and African-American culture.

USE SOCIAL SUPPORTS. Using social networks found in the family, neighborhood, church, mosque, temple, and community is how black women seek healing through others with similar experiences. Currently, many independent support groups for black women are being created around the country.

BUILD SELF-CONFIDENCE. This comes from action. Those who put forth effort to achieve their positive ambitions must overcome fear and work hard. Regardless of how successful we are in the end, it is our determination and sense of control that gives us confidence in self.

RECOGNIZE SYMPTOMS. No two people experience mental disorders in the same manner. Symptoms will vary in severity and duration among different people. For example, while feelings of worthlessness are a common symptom of depression in white women, changes in appetite are cited as a common sign of depression for black women.

DEVELOP AN ATTITUDE OF OPTIMISM. Those who think positively are greatly immune to the stress and feelings of depression common in everyday life.

MINIMIZE YOUR MENTAL STRESS. Most illnesses of the mind can be prevented by following the above steps on a daily basis so always practice being hopeful, forgiving others, and resisting stress.

Source: http://www.blackwomenshealth.com/Mental_Health.htm

On the first anniversary of my assault—and each anniversary since—I've celebrated my life and my healing. Despite that my attackers were never found, I have been able to overcome. I've journeyed so far so fast toward wellness because of my therapist, my boyfriend (now husband), my supportive family and friends, and divine healing. That's not to say I don't still face challenges from the attack. But what was done to me no longer has power over me.

PSALMS 94:17–19

Unless the LORD had given me help, I would soon have dwelt in the silence of death.

When I said, "My foot is slipping," your love, O LORD, supported me. When anxiety was great within me, your consolation brought joy to my soul.

PARTY POOPERS

Okay, so by now you've found that there are some people who made the guest list that shouldn't have or you've discovered that there are some uninvited, and, yes, unwanted, guests who have crashed your party. Like any hostess, you have the right to clean house even after the party has started. If there are people that you thought would support you and who have turned out to do the exact opposite, then you are within your rights to uninvite them to your party. That may mean just bluntly telling them that right now you need people that are positive in your life and you can't deal with their negativity. Or, you might quietly distance yourself from them until they get the hint. Just know that some people never catch the hint, and you may end up just telling them how you feel anyway. That's okay. You owe it to yourself and your healing to be honest with them. And you might help them learn things about themselves that they need to change.

But let's not forget the people who crash your party. You know the ones who claim that they want to help you but have turned out to be nothing more than a hindrance. There are also the ones that always turn your situation into their own personal dramas. Or, maybe they sound the alarms every time they do something for you because it's not about the action that they've taken but more about receiving recognition for having done it. Despite the performance that they put on, it becomes clear to you that they aren't really around to help you as much as they are to help themselves. I say, get rid of the dead weight.

Personally, I nip negativity in the bud, before it takes root. This takes me back to the time I'd attended a dance workshop shortly after I'd lost my first baby. I was feeling so good inside because it was my first time around a lot of sistahs since my miscarriage. I really needed to let loose, be free and get my dance on. But one of the ladies came over to bring in the dark cloud. (You know the type.) "Girl, you don't need to be doing all that jumping," she declared. "Didn't you just lose a baby three months ago?" Now if she knew about my loss, surely I knew about it. But I didn't trip. I politely ignored her and danced my anger out. I felt free and there was no way I was going to let her rain on my parade.

And others can be party poopers and not even know it. There were times when I'd be having a relatively good day and then someone would call and say "Girl, I heard you have cancer, I'm sorry. What did the doctors say?" Wrong question. They didn't even ask me how I was doing or if they could do anything before they probed for information. Were they concerned about helping me or just getting the scoop? It didn't matter either way, I'd just tell them that it's not a good time and I'd call them back later. Later, when I called them I would apologize for not being able to talk and tell them that rather than talk about cancer I'd like to talk about something else. They'd then apologize and change the subject. Now I do realize that maybe they didn't know what to say or do, particularly when they think someone is dying. And I think we owe it to them to let them know that it's okay: They can't be expected to have all the right words; nobody's perfect. At the same time, I'm not going to let anyone steal my joy. That's not an option.

So yes, there are party poopers who show up at everybody's gathering. The key is to be able to ensure that you don't let them and their own drama ruin what you have planned for your healing. Also, realize that people can provide different support at different times in their lives. Sometimes a one-time hug is all that one person has to give because of what's going on in their own life. Don't judge them, just deal.

I remember wanting a male family member of mine to be there for me. I honestly thought that he didn't love me because he barely called and didn't say much when he did. I was so hurt. Then I realized that he couldn't be there for me because he didn't know how to be there for himself. He loved me but he just didn't know how to show it. So rather than hold on to what he didn't do for me, I focused on what he did do. I forgave him for his shortcomings (Lord knows, we all have them). But most importantly, I learned how to be there for him, realizing that just because I'm going through things doesn't mean I can't take some time out to focus on someone else. Just as you shouldn't allow party poopers to integrate your life, you should also make sure that you don't become a party pooper in somebody else's life.

IT'S YOUR PARTY, CRY IF YOU WANT TO

Just because you're in fight mode, that doesn't mean that you won't have times of hurt, pain, and despair. Even when you enlist those you love to help you get through tough times, there will still be challenges, and there will still be times when you may want to give up.

It's alright to cry. Just don't cry for too long. Allow yourself some time and space to acknowledge your pain but just don't wallow in those feelings for too long. You've got work to do. And the only way you can get down to the business of healing is if you maintain a positive attitude and keep your support team close to your heart.

Step 3

Give It Up, Turn It Loose

Shellie after aerobics class

2/14/99

Truth be told, my ex-husband and I had problems from the start. But I always turned a blind eye to them.

I got pregnant the first week of our marriage. The first weekend of marriage he stayed out all night. I couldn't believe it. I felt worthless. And since I considered myself a payback woman, the battle was on. In response to his staying out all night, I decided I'd no longer behave as his wife . . . oh, it was ugly. We spent the bulk of our time doing things to piss each other off. Instead of making love, we made war over and over again. What a waste of precious time and energy.

Like me, my ex-husband had lots of resentment issues. His were with his mom; mine were with my dad. So, it's no surprise that we couldn't find love with each other, because we were both fighting the parents we begrudged every time we related to each other.

Today, I finally gave in and sought help. My friend who is a social worker asked me, "When you saw the train coming, why didn't you jump off the tracks?" That was a good question because I saw all of the warning signs indicating that my husband and I were headed nowhere fast. Yet I did nothing. I've been blaming my husband for everything bad that has happened to me since the day we met and that's not fair. My happiness isn't his responsibility—it's mine.

As the saying goes, it takes two to tango. That means everyone bears the responsibility when a relationship fails. But I never saw it that way. I blamed my ex-husband for all of the misfortune in our marriage. And after I lost my first child by him, I sought love from food, parties, and just hanging out. I was damaged and so incredibly angry that I couldn't keep my composure. Probably the most challenging part of the experience was that my anger wasn't just about the present, it was related to much of my past as well. So even though I still think it was messed up for my ex-husband to leave me on the day that I was diagnosed with breast cancer, if I focus on that alone, then I wouldn't be considering the whole story. Prior to that, my ex-husband really tried to make our marriage work. He even allowed us to move into an expensive apartment in hopes that we could salvage our marriage. But by that time it was too late for the both of us. We couldn't have a healthy marriage because we didn't even know what that meant.

The truth is that he needed to leave so that we could finally save ourselves. After he left, I gained the power to finally let go of my secret and told my godmother, Marie Williams, the truth about my relationship, my health, and my life. I needed to tell someone what was bothering me and I needed that person to tell me what to do with my feelings. She helped me realize that I needed to take care of myself, get a handle on my emotions, appreciate my spirit, and step into the present. My husband's departure allowed me to do that. If I continued to hold ill feelings toward him, then I would be ignoring the positive role he played in my life—one that is so important that it helped me become the woman, the wife, and mother that I am today.

Holding on to baggage that kept getting in my way was nothing new to me. Prior to breast cancer, I blamed my life's problems on everyone else. Even though I was nearly thirty years old, I was still mad at my father for not being a responsible parent. I had some ill feelings toward my mother because she raised me as a single parent. And again I blamed my ex-husband for most of the drama in my adult life. But breast cancer made me realize that blaming folks wasn't helping matters. Additionally, I needed to let go of past hurts and start taking responsibility for my own life. For true healing, I needed to forgive. Growing up in a single-parent home, the death of our child, his leaving, our divorce, and my renewal was all a part of the plan. If those things hadn't happened to me, I couldn't tell you how to overcome the trials that you face in your life.

As black women, we could find there are all types of things to complain about. Aside from the racism and sexism that many of us face on a regular basis, we also share other issues that commonly plague the black community. Many sisters are products of broken homes, single parents, underemployed, and underpaid. And then some of us have had people in our lives that we trusted with all of our hearts that just screwed us over for no apparent reason. It just doesn't seem fair but that's the way life is sometimes—unfair.

Now I'm not saying that you can't take some time out to have a good cry, go mad and scream at the top of your lungs, if that's what you need. When I was diagnosed with breast cancer, there was nothing pretty about my reaction and it certainly wasn't peaceful. I was mad as hell. I was scared as hell. I screamed. And I cried for several days straight. Like me, you may feel depressed, sad or mad. And you have every right to have those feelings because they are a normal part of the human experience. In addition, it's essential that you allow yourself to identify whatever emotions you're feeling so you can deal with them and move on. But that process shouldn't compel you to wallow in self-pity. Your feelings, if unmanaged, can serve as a hindrance if you allow yourself to be consumed by them. I soon realized that my crying, screaming and carrying on wasn't going to save my life. You also need to come to that conclusion.

My godmother, Marie, who is a social worker, says it's important to remember that being unforgiving does more harm to yourself than to the person you're harboring ill feelings against. "Let it go!" she insists. "When you feel that someone has wronged you, know that it will come back to them even though you may not see it. When I do something good for someone, I just do it. If it doesn't come back to me, it will come back to one of my children. And the same goes for when people do things to hurt other people, it comes back to them. The circle comes full."

LEVITICUS 19:18
Do not seek revenge or bear a grudge against one of your people, but love your neighbor as yourself.

So believe that those who wronged you will be dealt with some way, somehow—and move on. Besides, if you need to overcome a major challenge in your life, you have bigger and better endeavors to explore and you need to release any feelings of resentment you may be harboring if you want to experience true healing. Negative emotions can manifest themselves in very physical ways, by causing headaches, nausea, insomnia, and other illnesses such as cancer (believe me, I know). Also, feelings such as fear, tension, anger, or despair can prevent you from a successful recovery. The solution is to convert those harmful feelings into empowering ones, so you can start the healing process. Look for the lesson, not the loss. Here we'll find ways to discover recurrent themes in our lives so that we can assess close relationships and objectively evaluate whether they are fulfilling, release any resentment we feel against ourselves and others, learn to love everyone, accept mistakes—regardless of who makes them, let go of past guilt, and abandon evil thoughts or cynical or angry feelings.

Give it up, girlfriend. Turn loose those bad feelings that you may be holding against God, yourself, others, and the world so you can experience internal peace.

GIVING IT UP

At one time, giving things up was a real challenge for me. When I delivered my baby girl stillborn after six months, I blamed myself and had a really hard time letting those emotions go. I had never experienced a loss like that and I didn't have the tools for getting over the hurt. My mom, who was there to support me, was also at a loss. "I knew it was a lot for you to bear so I asked God to tell me what to say to you to help you go through it," my mom recalls. She says she needed to do something fast because she thought I was falling apart. She was right. So at her direction, the two of us scanned the local newspaper to find a church. Neither of us knew anybody in the church that we'd finally selected and had no idea what the sermon was going to be about. "And the preacher said that God has told him to preach on forgiveness. That sermon was directed right at you, Shellie. He told you to forgive yourself. You actually blamed yourself for losing your child and that's why you were taking the loss so hard. But once we heard that sermon, we both knew that God had given you permission to let that part of your life go. And that's why we both cried. What we didn't know was that another one of life's challenges would strike again in less than a year. If I had my way, I would have taken you right back home with me. But some things you have to let your children go through."

Breast cancer changed everything. Once I was diagnosed, I didn't have the opportunity to hold on to any negative things when I was told that I had two to five years to live. I didn't have time to put people under a microscope or alienate people who I didn't feel like being bothered with. I wanted to live and I learned to celebrate life. In short, I needed to start developing an *attitude of gratitude* (see Step 5) and listen to the lessons that my breast cancer was teaching me.

Forgiveness was key for me. I never knew how many people I didn't forgive until I sat down and took stock of my feelings. I took out a piece of paper and divided it into two columns. On one side, I wrote down all of the things that still caused me to have ill feelings. On the other side, I wrote a list of the people who I'd felt harmed me in some way—those people I hadn't forgiven. This included everyone from the gas station attendant to my junior high school teacher. I recorded things as small as an incident with a young lady from the telephone company, who'd called to tell me my phone was being cut off. Then I included a news organization on the list because I was still harboring ill will toward the employee who called me a black bitch. (It was hard for me to feel like I deserved to work there after that, so I never sought another job in the broadcast industry, even though that was my dream career.) Some of my aunts made the list for just being downright mean. The list also recorded larger transgressions like the ill feelings I held against my ex-husband for abandoning me. I even listed the president of the United States; I was ticked off at him and the U.S. government because I believed that they neglected my race by constantly overlooking our contributions. I blamed the government for all the pain and deaths that I associated with slavery. So, yes, the government made my list, too. Nobody was excluded, not even me. I blamed myself for not being smart enough and I was angry at myself for getting cancer. Once my columns were completed, I prayed for each situation and person that I included on that paper. I even personally called some people, just to make amends or just to let them know that I loved them. Now you might not believe this, but my list was so long that it took a whole year for me to forgive each person and release each incident that was on it. But I did it. And after I completed the process, I felt fifty pounds lighter.

A friend of mine is having a particularly challenging time dealing with what he sees as his dysfunctional family. According to him, they are abusive and have abused him in a lot of ways. Although he lived with his family until he reached adulthood, he now lives with his wife and her family and doesn't have any contact with the mother, father, and siblings he grew up with. He feels as though he has given them up and turned them loose, but unfortunately it's the opposite. Instead of letting go of the hurts that accompany his family memories, he remembers them well. He hasn't given up the pain. The thought never occurred to him that maybe God allowed him to have those childhood experiences so that he can be a source of light for those that are trapped in darkness. I am not saying that we must save the world or save all of our family members. But there are times when we should let go and let God come into our lives. Trust me once you forgive, God will send the people, or family members that need your light, and your experiences will be put into context.

Forgiveness allowed me to substitute some untruths I'd been holding onto along with some important truths. For example, I realized that while I was brought up to understand racism I never learned how to live beyond it. I was very angry and blamed all white people for the current state of the black race. I used to say that the reason we as a people aren't where we could be was because of racism. Now, I know differently. Yes, racism still exists but it's our beliefs that continue to keep us in bondage. I now trust God for making a place for my people *and* me.

Today, I know why Martin Luther King, Jr., had to fight a nonviolent fight. If he had not, our world would be so much different. As it stands now, his work helped make it possible for me to work with a major publisher so that, in order to help others, I could share my experiences, including the various challenges in my life. All of the opportunities we enjoy today are a by-product of the blood, sweat, and tears of those who made the big sacrifices so that this generation could have a better way. And we can't disappoint them. It's our responsibility to use these new freedoms to make the world a better place *by any means necessary* and to help others along as we forge ahead. My role in the scheme of things may be to use my trials and triumphs to inspire my entire family as well as the sisters of the world to live more emotionally and physically healthy lives, as we remember those who made the big sacrifices so that we could enjoy the rewards. No matter how bitter the world may become, I have an obligation to those that came before me, to the people that have yet to be born, and to myself to carry out God's will and complete the mission that He has designed for my life.

MATTHEW 6:14–15
For if you forgive men when they sin against you, your heavenly Father will also forgive you. But if you do not forgive men their sins, your Father will not forgive your sins.

There was another untruth I had to face: that parents aren't responsible for everything that takes place in their child's life. I had to stop being angry about growing up without my dad, because those feelings were destroying me. And they carried over into other things. I had problems forgiving people for making bad choices that affected kids, and I guess I felt that way because it reminded me of my own childhood. Not only as it related to me, but also as it related to some of my peers who acted out because they lacked attention. But how long can you blame parents for who you have become as an adult? You have forty-five-year-old men claiming that they can't be a father to their children because they grew up without a father. I say give me a break. At some point, we have to take responsibility for our own lives. Particularly since we are quick to blame our parents for the bad things that happen to us but never give them credit for the good things. I was guilty of this until I discovered the power of forgiveness.

You see my dad was my first love and when he and my mom separated, my spirit was broken. I always wanted to live with my father but I felt a huge responsibility to help my mom make due. I took on the role of helping Mom and I never forgave my dad for not being closer to our family and me. It was hard for me because he lived with us until I was ten years old. And I've always felt that his not being around hindered me from finding the girl, teenager, and woman that I longed to become. So I searched for love in some wrong places. But since I made the choice, I needed to bear the consequence. That's another one of those life lessons that I came to realize.

Now I have an awesome relationship with my dad. As a child, I never considered what he was going through. The truth was he had his own cross to bear. Back in 1974, he was diagnosed with kidney failure. He had to go on a dialysis machine (something he had never even heard of) when he was only thirty-two years old, requiring him to go on the machine for eight hours a day, three times a week, just to sustain himself. That meant it was impossible for him to keep a job or even conduct normal everyday activities without intense planning. So trips for any extended period of time require even more coordination to ensure that he gets his lifesaving treatment. He doesn't know what it's like to do something spontaneously because his life is dependent on a kidney machine that not only requires a substantial amount of time to use but drains him so much that a lot of his downtime is spent recuperating.

Some people would just give up under such dire circumstances, but my dad turned his life over to God and uses his experiences to inspire other people to sign their donor cards, learn how to read their medical records, and help get dialysis facilities in their areas. So far, he's responsible for over 238,000 new donor cards and he travels from city to city visiting various churches, health fairs, and organizations, encouraging people to give a second chance for life by donating their organs. He gets ten to thirty calls a day from people who need more information about dialysis and transplants. At age sixty, he has received two kidney transplants and is the oldest living renal patient in the United States. So far, he's had forty-one operations, including his two most recent surgeries in which he had to have his upper intestines and gall bladder removed because of gangrene. But, rather than get discouraged, he presses on: "I've been operated on forty-one times and have come out of every one of them. It was nothing but God," he beams. "I accept it. God healed me. He told me by his stripes that I was healed and I believed that. I can't add anything to it or take anything away from it."

And believe it or not, he still finds time to exercise (what's your excuse?). His routine consists of going to the gym every Tuesday and Thursday where he walks a mile around the track. That's what he does on days off from the dialysis machine, and, if he's feeling real good, he'll even work out on Saturday mornings.

When I think about everything that my father was going through and how much he actually has done for me I think he should be commended, not condemned. But it wasn't until I was thirty-two years old that I was able to tell him honestly that I loved him and that I really wanted a personal relationship with him. Prior to that, I held on to ill feelings about my dad and never thought he loved me. But that wasn't it; he could only give me what he had to give. When he showed up for my high school events, that was *his* way of showing his love for me. In fact, I realized that I didn't give him the credit he deserved: When I received an award for the most outstanding student in Baltimore from the mayor, he was there; when I received numerous awards for my athletic ability, my father was in the stands cheering me on. In fact, my dad came to every one of my high school achievements because he wanted to show me he cared. Sometimes we have to stop wanting people to love us the way we want them to and allow them to love us the way that they can.

Now if you believe that forgiveness follows some kind of a magical feeling, you're wrong! As personal coach Valorie Burton points out, you can feel angry or disappointed with someone, but that doesn't mean that your behavior has to show it. The way you act is a choice. "Sometimes you have to act your way into forgiveness," she explains. "You have to do what you know is the right thing to do even though it can be very difficult. You don't forgive because the other person is going to reciprocate it. You do it because you choose to forgive and because when you don't forgive, it eats away at you, even if you don't realize it. That anger or grudge that you have for the other person, impacts you. You'll find that the ill feelings that you're harboring spills over into other relationships and that's really not worth it."

And don't buy into the old saying "I can forgive but I can't forget," warn authors Linnie Frank and Andria Hall in their book *This Far by Faith: How to Put God First in Everyday Living*. According to them, that adage is nothing more than a hypocrisy. "This is where we sometimes bind our spiritual progress . . . we give rise to the opening of old wounds and the swelling of past hurts," they write, pointing out that if Jesus had the ability to let go of the memories of people who wronged him, so do we. "If we learn to truly forgive, we will notice that in time the details of betrayal, hurt, disappointment, and loss will fade, and just as surely, our hearts will expand to accept those who have failed us or let us down."

This forgiving piece is important and I took it very seriously. I wanted to really forgive, not just talk about it. It's the kind of forgiveness where once the person who wrongs you walks into the room, all you can do is offer them the same love and kindness that you would anybody else, because that's what they deserve as another human being. And that love and kindness that you're offering is sincere. You see, forgiveness was not about me; it wasn't even about the other person. I wanted to really forgive and forget so that God would extend that grace to me. So I dug deep to learn how to forgive my exhusband and other people in my life. And you know what I learned? When you learn how to forgive others, you also get to see what's wrong with you and how you've wronged somebody else. That was powerful for me.

ASKING FOR FORGIVENESS

Giving it up and turning it loose may also require that you eat crow—apologize to those people you've wronged. Yes, you have to own your stuff. And that's exactly what I had to do. As a start, I wrote a letter to my brother. I needed to have a rehearsal before speaking to him face-to-face. I wrote down everything I wanted to say so I wouldn't forget anything. I went back to when we were young. I was the oldest and we would argue because I felt like I was the boss. I would yell at him and sometimes make him feel bad. I would fight with him if he didn't do what I wanted him to do. After I got cancer, I felt guilty about how I treated him and felt I owed him an apology. I didn't forget the things that went on between and I figured he didn't either.

When I went to see him in Maryland, I asked him if we could talk and then we found a private space so I could tell him how I felt without interruption. I told him everything that I wish I hadn't done when we were kids. I apologized to him. He was gracious, telling me that he accepted that my actions were due to my youth and immaturity at that time. Even still, I told him that I was very sorry and that I wanted him to forgive me. I also told him that it was important for me to make amends because I wanted him to have my apology in his memory when he looked back on his childhood. He told me that he loved me and that everything was okay. More importantly, he said he forgave me.

TURNING IT LOOSE

God grant me the serenity to accept the things I cannot change.
Change the things I can
And the wisdom to know the difference.

One of the ways I've learned to turn things loose is to write down my feelings. If you're struggling to let something go, or even if you just have things on your mind that you want to express, I suggest keeping a journal or at least writing things down on scraps of paper (the good thing about a journal is that if you ever want to write a book, you'll have all of the information that you need in an organized fashion). Make the process of keeping a journal a project for *you*. Go shopping for a journal that represents your personality. Pick out your special pen and find a secure place to keep your notes. Don't edit when you're writing, just record your thoughts and emotions without worrying about grammar or the fear that someone else will read it. Then, from time to time, reread your notes. Sometimes you'll discover patterns. For example, you might find that you eat certain foods when you're feeling depressed, or maybe you'll find that your perceptions of things change as time passes: Things aren't as bad as they initially seem. In fact, your journal may become your best friend.

Talking about things also helps. If you can't talk to friends or family, connect with a psychologist or social worker. My godmother says that she couldn't let go of her brother until she found the courage to talk about his death.

My twin was killed in an automobile accident when we were both twenty-eight years old. That has been a terrible tragedy for me. As a big part of my work as a school social worker, I've counseled kids after their parents' deaths but death is still hard for me to deal with.

When I lost my twin, he was in the Navy at the time. And even though it's been forty-three years, it's still hard for me to talk about it. My daughters were five years old and sixteen months. The last time my brother came to visit me was around a holiday. I went to the door and then the two of us stood out on the porch. As he was going to his car and waving good-bye, I remember thinking, "What if I never see him alive again?" And I never did.

I remember asking God to get me through one hour at a time. Some people say to look at things day by day. But I tell people to ask God to give them the strength to get through each hour. I know I had to say a lot of prayers for strength to get over his death. I come from a family of nine children and he was the first to go. I had never experienced a death of someone that close to me. I would dream about him at least three times a week, but he was always alive.

I didn't know all of the things that I know now about death. I didn't become a social worker until twenty years later. So I didn't know what to do with the pain I was experiencing. But when I went to college, my feelings about my loss really came to the surface. I had the opportunity to write about a life experience to get credit. I wanted to write about my brother but it was too painful to explore. Then I took a course on death and dying and it was the first time I talked about my brother's death in public. All of the pain I'd been carrying was unleashed and I became hysterical in class. For so long, I'd pushed those feelings back but now I was opening up. Since my brother was divorced and we didn't have any contact with his family, my professor encouraged me to try to locate his children. I found his kids in California. It wasn't until I saw his

*son, who was the same age that my brother was when he died, that
I dreamed about my brother actually being dead. Then, I knew that
I had finally released him.*

Releasing is exactly what we all need to do if we are serious about
our healing. I have a friend who is very controlling. In fact, she is a
control fanatic. I remember that I asked her to do one thing with me
and, before I knew it, we were not only doing what she wanted but I
was also driving and paying for our outing. Her need to control her
surroundings is likely due to deep hurt or disappointment at some
point. Now she feels that she can prevent that pain from recurring by
staying in control. What she doesn't realize is that she is missing out
on more than she can ever imagine by preventing people from giving
to her. Being able to let someone else lead can be a very precious gift.
Unfortunately, she is letting her past hurts rule her. Like many of us,
she needs to give it up and turn it loose so she can start creating a
more fulfilling and liberating life.

I don't know what you need to do to turn loose those emotions or
memories that may be holding you back from enjoying your life to
the fullest. But whether it's talking to someone, writing down your
feelings, or just making a commitment to let something go, do whatever you need to do to experience true freedom. Your life is too important to let anything stand in your way. So get over that barrier as
soon as you can so you can prepare yourself for the victory that
awaits you.

Step 4

Get an Attitude of Gratitude

Shellie with her dad

2/20/00

"Oh no, Tony! Wake up, we lost the baby," I hollered. Blood was everywhere. I got up, called my friend Shakuwra and the three of us rushed to the emergency room. When we got there, the doctor couldn't find where the blood was coming from because the bleeding had completely stopped. When he did an ultrasound, the baby's heartbeat was strong and everything was normal. But I was still crying because I was afraid that my baby was going to die. I feared that I'd passed my cancer to my unborn child.

"We'll send you to your regular ob/gyn for a follow-up," he suggested. When that doctor examined me, he also couldn't find where *the blood was coming from. "But look," he said assuringly, "the baby is moving. You can hear the heartbeat. Shellie, the baby is fine."*

I know a clean bill of health from both doctors should have made me feel better but I was still anxious about the pregnancy. Three months later, I woke up at 4 A.M. and again there was blood everywhere. This time my friend Joy called and told me, "I don't know why I called, but it was like God told me to call you." She proceeded to pray over the phone while I was cleaning myself up. Tony was also praying. We waited until early that morning around 8 A.M. to see a doctor. Just as before, he couldn't determine where the blood was coming from.

After that, my pregnancy proceeded without any further difficulty. My son, delivered by C-section, was fine. He weighed ten pounds, two ounces, and was twenty-one inches long. He was beautiful. Two years later, when I was speaking to a spiritual sister of mine, I told her my story. "Are you sure you don't know where the blood was coming from?" she asked. I didn't. Then she continued, "Think, Shellie. It was the same time of morning with the same type of on again, off again. Shellie, you and Tony had been praying before Amir got here and you don't know where the blood was coming from?" I didn't have a clue. "God had to remove the blood that may have harmed the baby so he could be healthy. God performed a miracle for you and Tony, so you'd know that all children are born through him. There could have still been traces of chemo in your blood but God wanted Amir to live. Girl, you are blessed." And at that moment, I realized just how blessed I really was.

I didn't always believe I was blessed and highly favored by God (like I do now). At one time, there were so many things that upset me, I could barely keep track of them all. I didn't think I was thin enough. I was angry because my parents were divorced when I was only ten years old. I resented having to spend my teen years babysitting my younger brother. I begrudged my dad because he had the nerve to be sick with kidney disease during most of my childhood. I hated that my feet are a hefty size twelve. I wasn't as intelligent as I'd like to have been. I felt like my life was out of control. I hated my ex-husband for leaving me high and dry. I didn't think I was pretty enough. I wasn't sexy enough. I hated my career. I was unhappy with my salary. I felt that things never went my way. I wondered why I didn't win the lottery. I felt like I never got a break. I was disgruntled because I didn't think I got the respect I deserved. I didn't think anyone gave a damn about me. I couldn't stand my apartment. I hated my life.

Whew! Do any of these excuses sound familiar to you? I certainly hope not. If they do, you need to find a way to flush them out of your system because when I look back at all of the negativity I housed in my spirit, it's no wonder I got cancer. Even though I didn't complain outwardly, inside I was tearing myself down along with everything around me. I was living a lie. My face was smiling but my heart was bleeding. I ignored the anger that was building up inside as I continued to put up a front. I was fooling people, so I thought, while insisting that the life I was living was perfectly okay. Besides, I didn't think anything was wrong with me anyway: Everyone wears the game face to get through the day, don't they?

And maybe I did manage to fool people. As I interpreted my life, I concluded that things were all good. While my husband and I were living under the same roof, I was hanging with girls, dancing and partying, and laughing it up. But I was also lying to myself because I was really unhappy. Until I was diagnosed with cancer, however, I wasn't motivated to make changes in my life, especially as far as my attitude was concerned. It's unfortunate that I was never able to appreciate my life until I was faced with death. And despite my attempts to fool others, I was really being very foolish in my charade because, no matter what other people believed about me, I knew the truth.

Cancer forced me to develop a better attitude because I knew, if I didn't, my life would be over. As I also gained a closer relationship with

God, it became clear that if I didn't allow God to use me for his purpose that the enemy would use me for his—and to me that meant death. I hope you haven't waited as long as I have to develop an attitude of gratitude. As the old folks say, it's easy to complain about the shoes you're wearing until you meet a man that doesn't have feet. But even if you are currently holding on to negativity, you have a choice. As the Bible says, "Seek ye this day whom you will serve and all things shall be added unto you." You don't have to let your circumstances dictate your responses to them. On the contrary, a positive attitude will shape your approach to any situation that comes your way. As long as you count your blessings and try to seek the good in every scenario, including the tragedy that you now face, good will always reveal itself to you.

Please don't miss the point of this chapter, because an "attitude adjustment" is essential if you're ever going to overcome any of the challenges you face now or have yet to encounter. Just look at me. My attitude was the most important factor in getting a handle on my circumstances and influencing the results. With my bad attitude, I was forced to face a failed marriage, the loss of a child, deteriorating relationships, and a near fatal illness. But once I changed my attitude, my life made room for a happy marriage, a beautiful son, and healing. So I know firsthand, just how much a positive attitude can change your life. And my godmother (the woman who knows everything) agrees. "I think we have to remind ourselves that, in spite of what happens to us, there is always something to be grateful for when you look at the total picture," she says, insisting that staying grateful is something that she absolutely subscribes to. "In spite of what is happening in life, look at what you have to be grateful for. That's hard to do but it's still important."

In fact, I say having a positive attitude is a must. It's even more important than your American Express card. Don't leave home without it. Here's how you can get started on this stage of your transformation.

PHILIPPIANS 4:4–7

Rejoice in the Lord always. I will say it again: Rejoice! Let your gentleness be evident to all. The Lord is near. Do not be anxious about anything, but in everything, by prayer and petition, with thanksgiving, present your requests to God. And the peace of God, which transcends all understanding, will guard your hearts and your minds in Christ Jesus.

TURNING OVER A NEW LEAF

Nothing can inspire you to turn over a new leaf more than a near-death experience. But you shouldn't wait for that to occur before you change your outlook on your life. According to Dr. Grace Cornish in her book *10 Good Choices That Empower Black Women's Lives*, "We each have the ability to dismiss old beliefs, create new scenes, and cast new characters." In her book, she compares the mind to a personal safe-deposit box, one where only you have "the key to either open or close it, and to decide which thoughts to put in or take out."

If that is the case, then our view of the world really isn't based on our circumstance but what we choose to believe about those circumstances. That's why two people experiencing the exact same challenge can have totally different views about it and reactions to it. One claims victory, the other suffers defeat. One lives; the other dies. It's all a matter of the path that each of them has chosen to take. "There are many things in life that you won't be able to control . . . but you can control your reactions to them and manage your stress level accordingly," adds Cornish. That means your response to your current circumstance isn't a natural response but one that you have chosen to express.

In the book *This Far by Faith: How to Put God First in Everyday Living*, authors Linnie Frank and Andria Hall insist that our minds spend far too much time "looking for that which is bad for us or bad to us." Instead, they suggest we stop focusing on the obstacles before us and start thanking God for what he has brought us through individually and collectively. "Sometimes it's just a matter of the picture *you* paint of life; some people cast a dismal tint on everyone they come in contact with," they write, suggesting that we not only limit our exposure to negative people but that we also closely monitor the vibes that we're sending out to others. "We don't think about how far we've come. How we've grown. We think about what we don't have instead of being happy with what we've been blessed with. . . . We all can find something to be thankful for. It may be as simple as waking up in the morning, or eating a good meal, or seeing a loved one's smile. These are blessings and we should be thankful. And even in the toughest times when it's hard to find the good in a situation, just remember: God always makes a way. He always has, and He always will."

Our sister Debrena Jackson Gandy has some more news for you: "Attitude is not just a disposition or how you act; attitude is a state of mind and a state of heart." Once again, this indicates that you have control over your attitude and that you have the power to change it. Janice Lee experienced a string of misfortunes before she finally realized that it's not the challenge, it's how you go through it and what you draw from it:

The last fifteen years has been a crisis because it's been one issue behind another. It has resulted in changes in my lifestyle that have made it difficult to survive. I got married out of high school and had my first child at eighteen. I didn't start college until I was twenty-four years old and it took me thirteen years to finish. By age thirty, I had two children and had already gone through a divorce. As a result, I worked full-time as a single parent. I managed to go to school for my degree and get my boys through college with the help of my parents and my ex-husband. By the time I reached forty, I was pretty stable. But my brother, who had been a victim of substance abuse for many years, and his wife both contracted HIV. After my brother and his wife realized the situation they were in and my parents were not able to take on the full responsibility, I found myself in the midst of trying to manage that crisis. They ultimately died of AIDS. Two young children were left behind and I became their primary care-taker with the support of my parents. The idea of taking on that re-sponsibility after raising my own children really didn't appeal to me. Aside from threatening the relationship I had with my own sons, it came at a time when I had just graduated from school and landed an important position at the company where I worked. Juggling those new responsibilities was a difficult chore. I'd have to say that crisis was probably the most difficult trial I've faced.

I was not a happy camper when I realized those two little chil-dren came into my world. I was angry for a long time, and that was very apparent to everyone around me. I was just angry about life. Angry with the burden. Angry with having to be the responsible one. As far as I was concerned, I did all the right things, yet my brother wasn't accountable for his own actions and that caused me to have to take care of his responsibilities. But life's circumstances enabled me to take a step back and look at who I was and realize I wasn't happy about who I was becoming. I was able to step back and begin to recognize all of the gifts and blessings that were com-ing my way as a result of my having taken those boys. Initially, I took on that responsibility in a self-righteous way. But God bought those boys in my life so I could learn some things about myself and be closer to Him. The experience showed me that there was a God with powers far greater than I possessed. There were two very an-gry, wounded children and I can't tell you the effects of what hap-pens to families that have been victimized by drugs and what that does to the family structure. When you see children that are im-pacted by that at such an early age, it does something to you. Up until that tragic time, I'd always thought that I was the power behind my success, I'd overcome the stereotype of being a child bride, I got my degree, and raised my sons. It was all about me. When the boys came into my life, it became apparent that I couldn't do this alone. The emotion associated with the loss of my brother while trying to help those children survive and dealing with my parents was overwhelming. Yet, doors opened and people came to our aid in so many ways. If there is a time I can say that I believed in the power of God it was at that time. God continued to send angels to me with answers, resources, and solutions. I knew there was a God out there protecting me and guiding me while teaching me a strong lesson in humility. I learned to have love and compassion for other people. As a result, getting custody of my nephews was the best thing that ever happened to me.

Another tragic experience soon followed. Once I raised my two nephews for eight years, my second brother became very ill with heart disease. Dealing with him was a crisis as well as dealing with the fallout that occurred with my parents. My brother was critically ill and had two major heart surgeries. He tinkered with death for many years. When he became ill, it gave us a chance to go beyond the superficial relationship that we had and discover that we really cared about each other and loved each other very much. I think that the fear of losing a second brother without even knowing him was scary, and that forced me to work on my relationship with him. One of my issues with him was his drinking and how that impacted his family. I loved him enough to deal with that element and tell him how much I regretted how his alcoholism impacted our relationship. This enabled my brother and me to repair our relationship. Prior to that, there was always sibling rivalry between the two of us. I was the typical older sister; he was the brother that got in my way. I was critical of his lifestyle and he criticized my success. The prospect of death gave us a new appreciation for life in each other and we worked real hard to mend the bridge between us. My fondest days with him were when he was most critically ill. He died in June. Since he was my mother's companion, best friend, and caregiver, that loss has left a big void in my life and the lives of my parents. Since his death, my mother has become 98 percent blind and my dad is dealing with his own problems that come with aging. Thus, I'm in the midst of another crisis.

Through it all, I've learned so much. First, it's not what you're going through but how you go through it. I trust that there is a purpose, a role for me to play, and a lesson that I can take from it. I also realize that change has to begin with me. Whether my brother chose to deal with his alcoholism didn't matter, because I needed to work on my attitude and how I dealt with him so we could have a meaningful relationship. In addition, I found that you can't lose sight of the blessings that come your way in the midst of those storms. My brother could have died without my knowing him or trying to reconcile with him but that didn't happen. I couldn't avoid his destiny, but I could control the experience that I chose to take from my life with him. Finally, I learned not to put my life on hold until I got through the tragedy. Even through the hard times, I made the decision to work on my own dreams and I look forward to completing my doctorate. I could have continued to be the angry, hateful, mean woman that I was but I realized I had nothing to gain from that and instead focused on how I could use the experiences to grow.

Before you can change your attitude, you need to be clear on what about it needs to be adjusted. So take an honest assessment and ask yourself some questions:

- Are there any beliefs that you hold onto that really have no basis? For example, do you believe that *nothing* ever goes right for you? If so, take a good look at the assumption and try to find out if there is any basis for it. Think about all the things that have gone right for you. They can include big things like a promotion or small things like you were able to get to church on time last Sunday because you found a parking space close by. List all the points that come to mind and see how they disprove the point that "nothing" ever goes right for you. Even if your list is short, that's still *something*. And if you truly can't find *anything* that goes right for you (which seems next to impossible), then make a concerted effort to change your approach so you can get better results. The point is to change your assumptions in order to alter your attitude.

- Are you stuck in a "keeping-up-with-the-Joneses" mode? If you always want what someone else has, then you will never be truly happy because you're relying on external forces to bring you joy, and those factors are forever changing. Besides, "true contentment can only come from within," cautions Cornish, "outside escapes may supply temporary joy, but they have no lasting influence." Just know that the life designed for you is one that was specifically customized by God. If you're continually focused on other people's lives, you'll miss the wonderful gifts that God has in store for you. Instead of being envious of others, be happy for them and be confident in knowing that for every season there is a reason—your harvest will soon arrive.

- Are you always playing defense? Change your position, sis. If you want to win in the game of life, you need to view the playing field from all angles. If you're always ready for the attack, then you'll always be in the midst of a battle. Give people the benefit of the doubt and assume they're innocent until you've received proof that they're guilty. Also, don't hold anyone responsible for sins that were committed by someone else. In other words, if

SHELLIE'S ATTITUDE ADJUSTMENT PLAN

WHY I HAD A POOR ATTITUDE:	WHAT I DID ABOUT IT:
I don't think I'm thin enough.	Looked at myself in a full-length mirror until I learned to embrace every dimple and roll. I constantly told myself that I was beautiful and changed my mind-set: "So what if I don't look like the people I work with; beauty is not what you see, it's who you are."
Irritated with my parents for not staying together	I realized that life is full of ups and downs. I asked God to help me forgive my parents for making choices that I didn't think were best for my brother and me. Not only did God reveal to me the reason why the separation occurred when it did, He also warned me against judging my parents. If I continued down that path, I'd run the risk of having my son judge me for my mistakes. And more importantly, I realized that I couldn't ask God to forgive me for my transgressions if I couldn't forgive the very people that brought me into the world.
Angry with my brother for my having to watch him when we were young	I got over it. He was just a kid and it wasn't his fault.
Bitter with my dad for being sick	I just concentrated on loving him. How could I not? He is so strong that he is the longest-living dialysis patient in the world. Now I'm proud of my superdad. I also called him one evening to ask him if he was open to us having a more personal relationship, because I wanted to learn to love him more.

Annoyed with the fact that my feet are too big

I learned to be grateful for my feet because they support a truly great woman. When I was ten years old I wore a size ten in women's shoes and was the laughingstock in elementary school. When my mother would take me to get shoes, I had to buy grown-up shoes. Not the shoes that young girls wore. When the other kids looked ten I looked fifteen. I was always embarrassed but then as my body grew taller and taller, I realized that my big feet were essential.

Frustrated because I had no self-control over what I ate

All of my life I have been a pretty healthy woman. But I have been at war with my body for years when it comes to managing my diet. That made me angry because my butt was big and stuck out. But when I started teaching aerobics to a slew of women who looked just like me, I stood as an example that large women could also be healthy women. My students, who ranged from fat, skinny, short, tall, frail, thin, big-hands and big-feet women, enabled me to accept my body and I helped them to accept theirs. God doesn't make mistakes; we're all perfect in his sight. He loves us beyond what we weigh. Instead of continuing to be at war with myself, I learned to love every single ounce of me.

Unforgiving with family members

There is a lot of talk about a generational curse. I believe we can also pass down generational anger. Once I realized this truth, I vowed to stop the hate. As a child, I watched relatives backbite and gossip about people all day. It wasn't an uplifting or a positive example for my adult development. They were on a mission to tear each other down. Although I could have continued to carry the baton for the next generation, I was determined to end the vicious cycle that had become a part of our family tree. I pruned the weeds of jealousy, bitterness, and failure. I still chose to love my family and accept them at whatever level they were on. But I stopped participating in the negativity.

Unhappy because I held on to past guilt	I simply had to let go and let God, so I could release myself of things I'd done in the past that constantly haunted my spirit. I learned that bad memories keep us from being grateful. My pastor at my church taught me that. I could pray and ask God to forgive me and constantly pray about that which I'd done wrong so that I did not repeat it. As long as I stayed prayerful, that helped me to stay on the right path.

person A "done you wrong," don't take it out on person B. It's not her fault, and she deserves to be treated as an individual.

- Are you forever a victim? Contrary to what people believe, everyone has his or her share of ups and downs. But outcomes vary widely because your attitude can influence your perception of a situation, shape your experience, and can alter the outcome of a particular scenario. Instead of taking the "woe is me" approach, start ensuring that your reasons for success far outweigh your reasons for failure.

- Are you exuding negativity? If you don't know, find out. Some clues to look for are constant complaining, chronic bickering, poor performance appraisals, involvement in various disputes, a loss of friends and family relationships, bad language (including excessive use of profanity), and deteriorating self-esteem. Any of these things requires an immediate attitude adjustment so you can change the impact you have on yourself and others.

MAKING THE ADJUSTMENT

Okay, so now you've identified some areas that you need to change if you want to get an attitude adjustment. But if you're serious about

PRAYER OF THANKSGIVING

Life coach Paula McGee, who is also president of Paula McGee Ministries, a non-profit organization whose vision is to "inspire every woman to recognize, accept, and fulfill her call to greatness," has personally developed a prayer for thanksgiving. If you're going through tough times, McGee says this prayer will at least momentarily allow you to focus on God's goodness instead of the tragedy you now face.

DEAR GOD,

I am thankful for all of the blessings you have provided for me.

I know that you have called me to do this work and to be blessed.

I accept that I am created in your image and claim that greatness. (GENESIS 1:27)

I accept that I am a part of a chosen generation, a royal priesthood, and a peculiar people. (1 PETER 2:9)

I am your child and a joint heir with Jesus. (ROMANS 8:17)

I accept that I have full access to all of your glory.

I accept that you can do exceedingly, abundantly, above all that I can ask or think through the power that is working in me. (EPHESIANS 3:20)

I accept that you have blessed me that I might be a blessing to others.

I believe that you will lead and guide me—that you will provide all that I need according to your riches in glory. (PHILIPPIANS 4:19)

You have made me, like David, Moses, Deborah, and Esther, to be a leader. I accept this fully.

I am not afraid to be who you have created me to be.

I will always operate in faith and not fear. For you have not given me the spirit of fear, but of love, power, and a sound mind. (2 TIMOTHY 1:7)

Your son Jesus is the author and finisher of my faith. (HEBREWS 12:2)

Thank you for perfecting my faith.

Now, God, lead and guide me, for I am committed to do this work.

I am an example of your goodness, your grace, and your mercy.

I give you all honor and praise for my life and my gifts.

My will is to do your will and to fulfill my divine purpose.

Have your way in my life!

In Jesus' name I pray.

AMEN

RECOGNIZE YOUR GREATNESS

You can have an attitude of gratitude when you realize how great the creator has made you and what gifts you have at your disposal. In addition, the tragedy before you might seem less overwhelming if you recognize that you already have every-thing you need to deal with it. Read these words as a reminder:

Our deepest fear is not that we are inadequate. Our deepest fear is that we are powerful beyond measure. It is our light, not our darkness, that most frightens us.

We ask ourselves, who am I to be brilliant, gorgeous, talented, and fabulous? Actually, who are we not to be?

You are a child of God. Your playing small does not serve the world. There is nothing en-lightened about shrinking so that other people won't feel insecure about you. We were born to manifest the glory of God that is within us.

It is not just in some of us; it's in everyone.

And as we let our own light shine, we unconsciously give other people permission to do the same. As we are liberated from our own fear, our presence automatically liberates others.

Marianne Williamson as quoted by Nelson Mandella in his 1994 inaugural speech.

making a change, you can't stop now. You've got to keep the ball rolling by substituting those new habits for older ones. The change won't happen over night but what do you expect, you didn't develop those attitudes overnight either.

Let's start by finding constructive ways to express your anger and dismay. Yeah, you'll still get angry, ticked off even, but you need to find better ways to handle it. Hear this: I'm not saying that just be-cause you've changed your attitude that you give people a free pass to walk over you. On the contrary, once you've changed your attitude you'll feel better about yourself and you'll value yourself. So being mistreated isn't an option.

At the same time, communicating your dismay still requires protocol. You can't just tell folks to just go to hell, like you did in the past. Partially because you understand that what you do and how you treat people is not just about you but about how you represent the higher power in His divine plan. Even when people downright piss you off, you have an obligation to take the high road and shine in the face of adversity. That's just who you are. With your new attitude you won't cuss people out—partially because it just doesn't look good for you to be doing that, but mostly because once you change your attitude and cleanse your spirit, you won't even want to do that because that type of negativity no longer reigns in your heart. Once you get an attitude of gratitude, you'll care too much for yourself to let anyone prevent you from acting like the divine woman that God made you to be. If that sounds too good to be true, then that's all the more reason to make a change.

But back to finding ways to give constructive feedback. An article in *Heart & Soul* magazine (October 2003) argued that complaining could actually be bad for your health because the high stress you endure from being a chronic complainer could lead to conditions such as hypertension, diabetes, and cancer. It suggested the following approach for nixing the negativity but still giving someone a piece of your mind in a classy, but I-mean-business, type of a way:

Be real about your condition. If you find yourself complaining or raining on other people's parade, be honest about it. Apologize and make a real effort to stop spreading bad vibes.

Count your blessings. That's what this whole chapter is about. But if it takes counting them one by one, just do it. The point is that once your realize just how good God has been to you, you'll be hard-pressed to keep up a negative aura.

Connect with your spirit. Draw positive energy through meditation and by surrounding yourself with positive people.

Change your environment. As I said before, I gave my apartment a facelift and changed my routine so I could change my outlook. It really helped.

Ask for support. We've already tackled this area. But while you're asking for help, also ask your friends and family for feedback, insisting that they check you if you resort to your former negative ways.

Wrong the rights. Again, if you need to set something straight with someone, do it. And if you're holding bad feelings toward someone who has offended you, just let it go.

Seek the truth. When I reached out to my father to improve our relationship, he reminded me of all of the times that he has been in my life. Over the years, he'd attended all my special events. He wanted to do more but his illness wouldn't permit it. I was so busy being bitter that I really never considered his perspective. When you don't have an attitude of gratitude, it's easy to forget the good that people have done. Instead, you hold on to notions and ideas about the person that feed into your negative image of them. After communicating with my dad, I realized that not only did he love me but he has been reaching out to me all of my life. I just failed to reach back.

Celebrate. You may not feel like celebrating now and that's understandable. But when there is a more appropriate time, celebrate your new attitude. It doesn't have to be anything big, but you should do something. By providing yourself with positive reinforcement, you'll want to continue on your path of self-discovery and self-love.

DEUTERONOMY 7:9
Know therefore that the LORD your God is God; he is the faithful God, keeping his covenant of love to a thousand generations of those who love him and keep his commands.

KEEPING IT REAL

Don't think that making a change means that you have to let go of your authentic self. It's just the opposite, changing your attitude requires you to become the best woman that you can be. The difference between the old you and the new you will be someone who is ready to do whatever it takes to claim the victory over life's latest blow.

For Gandy, keeping it real means accepting the seasons of life and developing strategies to deal with them:

We tend not to do too well with tragedy because we've created a culture of images and illusions that are perfect. We tend to view things as an "Alice and Wonderland" type of perfection. But just like our world, we have seasons in our lives. We tend to see our lives in summer, always having fruit, and that's why we're often not very equipped to deal with fall and winter. We find it harder on us because we are only prepared for summer. So we deal with the changes in our lives by kicking and screaming, trying to resist it. But change is unavoidable.

In our lives, the season of fall looks like breakdown. You'll see things falling apart. It might be a relationship, a job situation, our bodies might have some physical challenges, or our business might lose some big contracts. Our fruit starts falling off, and it is going into decay. Winter is a time of stillness. To the eye it looks like things have stagnated completely. You might find that you are making calls and getting no returns. On the dating scene, maybe you are going to more parties than ever and trying to meet a mate by putting an ad in the newspaper, but you still aren't getting any action. That's a sign you're in winter. You can't fight the season; it's a natural cycle that's bigger than any of us. The four cycles— fall, winter, spring, and summer—affect every living thing. If we know what some of the characteristics are, we can recognize when those seasons come into our lives. Every season is needed. We couldn't go from summer to winter. Yet, we try to jump over fall and winter and stay in spring and summer but it creates a tremen- dous amount of pain if we don't try to work through it in our lives.

Winter is a time for stillness. And if you don't recognize that, you'll burn yourself out. During your winter, I say chill out, relax, go within, feed your spirit, contemplate, reflect, keep a journal, meditate, and pray. Otherwise, you'll find that the season lasts longer if you don't let it have its place. We've worked against our natural seasons for so long that our bodies and our minds are freaking out when it occurs. But seasons are a natural part of just being.

Winter people tend to move slower and go places late. If you're in winter, things around you look barren but there are all kinds of things going on beneath the surface and that coincide with our lives. The only difference is that the seasons in our lives don't neces- sarily coincide with the weather. Our own seasons could last for years, months, days, or various time frames. If we can recognize that all four seasons are part of life, and become intimate with all four seasons, we wouldn't suffer so terribly and hugely when tragedies come.

Ready for a full transformation? Then you've got to get ready to work, sis. So far, you should have made an assessment of the things about your attitude that you need to change, started developing an attitude adjustment plan by using my own plan for guidance, and developed constructive ways to better communicate with the people around you. So what's left? Add these points to your to-do list:

- Check out the recurrent themes that keep emerging in your life. Take a real good look at the things that are happening to you, including as they relate to this latest challenge. List the things that keep showing up for you. For example, do you find that you're always late or running behind schedule? Remember, latecomers only get the leftovers, it's the early birds that have an opportunity to choose from the full selection of offerings—stop settling for leftovers. But there may be other areas that are standing in your way. Maybe you're constantly borrowing or lending money. Or maybe you find yourself going from one emergency to another. These things may seem like you have absolutely no control over them but maybe your attitude and your belief system are making room for these weeds to take root in your life. Identify them and find ways to eliminate them.

- Assess close relationships and objectively evaluate whether they are fulfilling. There are people in our lives that we've known since forever and we think that they always have to be in our lives. That's not necessarily so. Some people come into our lives for a reason—for a season or a lifetime. As you move through your transformation, determine which relationships should remain the same, change, or just be eliminated altogether. As you know, people say and do some angry vicious things to one another. They can be mean, selfish, and afraid. I assess my relationships based on where I want to go in my life and I let my behavior support my belief system. Remember, people who have the same interests are attracted to the same types of activities and that's how relationships are formed. If you are a drinker, for example, you and the people you associate with may like to hang out in bars. If you are an athlete, you'll make the most of your associations at sports-related activities. By the same token, if you are a church lady, then you should draw people that are prayerful, if you are indeed in the right church. So the bottom line is that if you don't like the friendships that you're making, you probably need to change your meeting place—hang out someplace else.

Harriette Cole, author of *Choosing Truth: Living an Authentic Life,* offers other advice about assessing friendships in her book. She says you can determine which friendships are authentic by simply observing and evaluating your interactions with your associates. Suggesting that each of us has the inner wisdom to guide us in these decisions, she writes: "Look at what people say, and notice what they do. When you envision yourself as worthy of respect and honor, you will attract respectful and honorable relationships . . . Be vigilant about your friendships. Be kind and respectful toward others and compassionate toward everyone, including yourself. Notice when a relationship sours, and have the courage to let go."

- Release resentment. Unless you've skipped Step 3, you should have already learned how to give things up and turn them loose.

- Flip the script. In Dr. Grace Cornish's book *10 Good Choices that Empower Black Women's Lives,* she charges readers to write their own script. She writes: "At birth, we were handed a script prepared by a self-appointed playwright. Throughout our life experiences, we have to enact many unsuitable and unhappy scenes. But nowhere in our individual scripts is it written that the script cannot be changed." She is right. We don't have to absorb the beliefs, myths or lies that we have been taught; we can reeducate ourselves. We don't have to keep going down the same hill of frustration and regret, we can chart a new course. We don't have to buy into other people's perception of us or our situations. We can define ourselves. And we don't have to continue to look outside of ourselves—at other people, places and things—for happiness. We can tap the joy within by discovering our secret to peace and self-preservation. Start by making a list of the things that bring you joy and commit doing at least one of those things every day. When you run out of things to do, start over and add to your list on a regular basis. Just remember, as Cornish writes, "outside escapes may supply joy temporarily, but have no lasting influence. True contentment can only come from within."

- Let go of past guilt and accept the mistakes that were made—by you or others. No matter what it is that you're going through, it's important that you let go of whatever guilty feelings you may be holding onto regarding the situation. Even if it is your fault, pointing fingers isn't going to change things. And sometimes we never find out whose fault it is, and it really doesn't matter. "We're a society that needs and likes to have answers but there aren't any answers as to why bad things happen to us," states psychotherapist Julia Boyd, who goes on to say that a lot of times a number of factors contribute to a bad situation. "Its hard to pin it on one thing," she adds. "Sometimes magic happens but sometimes it doesn't." We just need to be able to deal with the outcome regardless of the results.

- Know that life is for the living. This sounds obvious but some people spend their whole time on earth as "dead men (or women) walking." I know because when I was first diagnosed with cancer, a lot of them came out of the woodwork and I'll tell you, if I hung out with them, I wouldn't be here right now. There are people who whiz through each day without ever really having an appreciation for it and they never take any time out to enjoy it. What a waste. Believe me, if you take the time out to notice every second, minute, and hour that God has blessed you with, there is no way you can't have an attitude of gratitude. Don't let life pass you by—and realize right now that this isn't a dress rehearsal. It's the real thing. You won't get another chance to make the most out of the life you have now. So cherish the moment, make the most of it, and surround yourself with other people who are on this earth to truly live their lives to it's fullest potential. And, yes, I know things may look grim now, but you have the opportunity to redefine the next moment by simply changing your attitude. If not now, then when? Tomorrow may never come.

Step 5

Exercise for Healing

Shellie with Kecia Palmer Cousins and Tracey Adams

3/10/96

I don't want to get up. I am so angry with my body. Why do these women even come to my class? Don't they see that I am struggling with my own weight? It's not like I'm the ideal fitness instructor. I don't have the long sexy legs or small waist with the bomb measurements of 36–24–36.

I just feel really sluggish. I guess that box of cookies I ate before I went to bed was a bad move. I eat when I'm depressed, but when I eat the wrong foods, I feel worse. This is definitely not the way I want to start my day. The fact that I'm not taking care of myself is obvious. And I don't want these women to think I'm not happy with myself—even if it's true. I've admitted to them that I'm struggling with my weight but I haven't confessed that I'm also just struggling with me. Struggling to be me. Struggling to just get up in the morning. Maybe we can find a way to take care of one another. Or maybe there's something to this exercise thing. They say there is a mind-body connection. I'm beginning to believe that there is some truth to that.

I just know that when I get in there and shake my thing, it's like a natural high. The more I move, the more I want to move because I notice that the sick feeling that I get from chemo is starting to disappear. The bitter taste in my mouth is fading away and I'm getting stronger.

I recently spoke to another cancer survivor who asked me why I chose to teach aerobics while I was going through chemo. I told her if it were up to me, I would go home and relax, just like the doctor ordered. But that just isn't God's will for me. He requires more, so I just have to give more.

I now know there is no emotional healing without physical healing for me. My body requires it. Aerobics saved my life. My energy shot up and that made me feel better. Plus, the sweating helped me release the toxins that the chemo left behind. Through my experiences, I've learned what exercising on a regular basis does to your moods and your emotions. It provides a natural high.

But aerobics isn't just good for cancer survivors. Any form of exercise is essential for good health and stress relief. Apparently we sisters don't know the power of exercise since four out of ten black women don't participate in "leisure-time physical activity" according to a 1992 Centers for Disease Control and Prevention survey. We're also less likely to exercise than black men and white women.* In addition, black

---

* Linda Villarosa, *Body & Soul: The Black Woman's Guide to Physical and Emotional Well-Being* (New York: HarperPerennial, 1994), p. 34.

women offer all types of excuses when asked why they don't exercise. Many view it as stressful and have never understood the relationship between exercise and good health. But our sedentary lifestyle is killing us, and if you are going through a tragedy a well-balanced exercise program may be more of an immediate need for you.

The mind can definitely rule the body as long as we learn how to make the right connection. Sis, I know we can be so entrenched in what's going on in our lives that we can forget about our bodies, but I want to remind you that they need special attention. If you want to keep moving forward, you must lubricate the joints, stretch all of your parts, and learn to breathe.

Do you have a full-length mirror around? If not, borrow one and really check yourself out. It's not about body type, because whether you're fat, skinny, tall, full-figured, obese, thin, slim, or short, you have to work out. Your body requires it if you want to maintain your best physical health. Otherwise diseases such as diabetes, cancer, and osteoporosis, can sneak into your life.

Have you found that mirror yet? Good. Now make a promise to the woman looking back at you that you're going to take good care of her and make a commitment to do it today.

In this chapter we look at all of the reasons why you say you don't exercise and tell you why those reasons don't hold up. In addition, this chapter features a comprehensive exercise program and will reference an exercise regimen designed specifically for survivors, a program that includes walking, stretching, low-impact aerobics, and facial movements.

Further, the chapter discusses the emotional exercises that black women should practice, which includes loving others; smiling constantly; forcing yourself to be happy when you're feeling low; telling the truth; reading the Bible; hanging around positive, confident people; and laughing regularly. Sounds easy enough? Then let's get with the program.

EXERCISE EXCUSES THAT DON'T HOLD WATER

Even I had my own personal myths and misconceptions about fitness, especially since I had cancer. But once I heard the music at the aerobics class and once I allowed myself to enjoy the feeling, I started moving and the spirit took over. My energy and my love for dance emerged. I didn't know it at the time, but I really think I used aerobics as the first challenge in my recovery. I was involved in a fight between my body and myself. Had I not gone through this exercise, I would have allowed the cancer to beat me, and that's a fight I wasn't ready to lose. Back then, I didn't know what I was doing. It was about living emotionally, surviving, and forcing myself to keep believing in life. I had to be stronger than the false beliefs I had about exercise and so do you.

The media still perpetuates the belief that the blond-haired, blue-eyed thin woman is the ideal American beauty. But that doesn't have to be our belief, we should know better. Let's look at the many common stereotypes that society places on women of color as it relates to their body image as well as the reasons why these misconceptions don't hold up:

- **Most aerobic instructors are thin.** As a full-figured woman weighing two hundred fifty pounds at five feet, nine inches tall, I am often underestimated by the newcomers in the aerobics classes that I teach. But, after a few sessions, the students realize that, despite my size, I'm light on my feet. In fact, I'm always the most popular aerobics teacher no matter where I teach. I thank God for allowing me to be physically capable of inspiring others to be motivated to be fit at any size. You don't have to be thin to exercise or teach aerobics. You just need to be ready, willing, and able to make the commitment to better health.

- **Full-figured women don't have energy.** It's true that people who are overweight tend to have less stamina because they are carrying excessive weight. But, it's also true that slim sisters who don't exercise on a regular basis are equally as challenged by a thorough aerobics program. You'll find that exercising becomes easier as you increase its frequency. So, don't get discouraged if you start exercising and find that you're completely wiped out. It happens to all of us at first. But, if you continue to exercise, gradually increase the frequency and intensity of your exercise program, you'll become more energized. And that doesn't matter if you're full-figured or not.

- **Full-figured women aren't lovable.** Says who? Whoever said that certainly hasn't come into contact with the likes of Star Jones, Mahalia Jackson, Nell Carter, Della Reese, Queen Latifah, Oprah, and Aretha Franklin. These women contributed to American society in ways that could not be measured or confined. They are not only treasured by their fans and admirers, they are also loved by their families and friends. If you're a full-figured woman, you can be loved by everyone around you as long as you first love yourself.

- **Women who go through tragedy can't exercise.** When I lost my child in 1994, aerobics kept me feeling like my body still belonged to me. Exercise also became my stress relief from an angry and bitter marriage. For example, I would go to the Mount Vernon YMCA after heated arguments with my husband. When I came home, I wouldn't have a clue as to why we argued in the first place, and the problems that my husband and I were having weren't as bad as I thought. Through exercise I was able to change my feelings about life and its issues and challenges. Exercise made me feel like I could still go on.

  Aside from the health benefits, exercise is also a great stress buster. That's why my godmother, Marie Williams, makes sure she walks five miles two or three times a week and attends a Curves class four times a week. Her regular workouts continue even when she goes through life's challenges. "Back in 1997, I lost a niece, sister, and brother all in the same year," she reminisces. "There were many days I walked with tears streaming down my face but I continued to walk and it got me through the day."

I think you'll find that exercise can help you, too. Now, I know tragedies are tough and they can sap your time and energy. But that can only happen, if you let them. Going through a tough time doesn't mean that you should submit to it. On the contrary, a tragedy should illustrate the importance of life. And it's much too important to live your life without any concern for your health and wellness. You owe it to yourself as well as the people you support to be as healthy as possible, and that requires that you make time to exercise. Now, maybe you'll find it difficult to maintain a regular gym regimen, but you should always make time to take a brisk walk, stretch, run in place, lift weights, and eat right. Not only will this help make tragedy easier to bear, it will help you think more clearly, so you consider the world of possibilities that God has put before you.

So that's what society says about exercise. What do you say? I bet you believe you have good reasons why you don't exercise and they don't necessarily have to do with the particular tragedy that you're facing. Your reasons for not exercising have more to do with your busy life. But just like the excuses we discussed, they also don't hold water. Here's why:

- **"I don't have enough time to exercise."** Of course you do. No matter what you do or where you are, you can exercise throughout the day. Take a twenty-minute stroll during a break or lunch. Or maybe you'll just want to do stretching exercises at your desk. If you're really motivated, you can get up an hour earlier for some high-impact aerobics or a jog. You can also do little things like park your car further away from your destinations so you can get in the habit of walking more frequently. As we said earlier, the point is to start exercising even at a basic level with the goal of gradually increasing the frequency and intensity of your regimen.

- **"I don't like exercise."** That's impossible. You have to like some type of exercise because it comes in so many different forms. You can even get a workout from everyday activities like shopping, housecleaning, gardening, or playing with your kids. As a start, try finding ways to increase your heartbeat when participating in your daily activities. Concentrate on finding things that you enjoy and you'll increase the likelihood of your long-term participation in them.

- **"I'm too overweight to exercise."** You're never too overweight to exercise. In fact, people who are overweight are great motivators to others. As pointed out by author Monique Brown in her book, *It's a Sistah Thing: A Guide to Understanding and Dealing with Fibroids for Black Women:* "You'll enjoy the added flexibility, stamina, and strength that exercise promotes. And you'll feel better about yourself because you're finally taking responsibility for your own happiness and well-being."

- **"I'm too tired."** Join the club. Anyone who has ever experienced a tragedy can attest to the lifelessness that results. Still, forcing yourself to exercise will help you feel less tired because physical activity inspires mental alertness as well as stimulates the brain's production of mood-enhancing chemicals such as neurotransmitters and endorphins.

Any other reasons for not exercising? Take out a piece of paper, make a list, and check it twice. Then for every reason you have for not exercising, write down reasons to combat that excuse. Before you know it, you won't be able to find one good reason for not starting an exercise program.

EXERCISE, EATING, AND ENDURING

Sisters, don't think that you can enjoy the benefits of exercise without eating right—the two go hand in hand. Time and again, I realize that I'm a great exerciser but a poor dieter. And I deal with this struggle on a daily basis. But, because exercising has stimulated feelings of self-love, I know that I'll overcome this challenge as well.

You see I've always relied on yo-yo dieting as a means to manage my food intake. But that only promoted low self-esteem because the results of those diets were temporary. You can't keep doing the same things, if you want different results. So, I'm committed to eating differently as a way to achieve a change over the long haul.

In Monique Greenwood's book, *Having What Matters,* she talks about how she learned to view food differently. "Instead of living to eat, I eat to live," she writes, confessing that she gave up pork in the late 1980s when her husband refused to kiss her after she'd eaten a pork chop. "He knew early on that pork and too much red meat can lead to high cholesterol and clogging of the arteries. A high-fat diet has also been linked to certain forms of cancer," she adds.

As a suggestion, she recommends along with her trainer Duvall, a few dietary rules that include: cutting down on the carbohydrates such as potatoes, pastas and breads; flushing out your system with at least eight to ten glasses of water a day; eating something before you start your workout; eating more often but just picking healthier foods such as salads (minus the fatty dressing), fruits, vegetables, grilled or baked fish; and snacking smart by eating foods with low calorie counts and high health benefits.

PUTTING A PROGRAM INTO PLAY

What's keeping you from working that body? Absolutely nothing. As Greenwood points out in her book, exercise helps you to transform your mind, body, and spirit. "Since I began to work out regularly, I'm loving the body I'm in—not just because my size twelve frame is trimmer and my husband thinks I'm all that, but because I know this is the best me I can be," she writes. "The most satisfying feeling of all comes from those sacred sixty to ninety fitness minutes of oneness with myself. The actions of my body somehow work to magically transform my mind and my spirit. I'm filled with a sense of control and accomplishment that is quite unlike anything I've ever experienced . . . My devotion to exercise has taught me a valuable lesson: Sometimes what's good *for* you is also good *to* you."

Kecia Palmer Cousins agrees that exercise is essential for both physical and mental well-being. She started her company, Aerobic-soul Incorporated, after participating in an aerobics class that I taught at the YWCA in Yonkers. According to her, participating in exercise on a regular basis has been a life-altering event for herself as well as her students:

If you'll recall Shellie, I met you the week that you were diagnosed with cancer. I used to host slumber parties for young girls at my house; the gatherings were partially for fun and partially to focus on career and education. So from Friday through Saturday, the young ladies would be in store for an empowering weekend during which women from the community would stop by to talk to them. One of the people I invited was Marie Williams, and she brought you to my house that night as her guest. She wanted to cheer you up. Given the circumstances, I thought you had a great attitude.

So when you started teaching aerobics, I started taking your classes to stay fit and support your business. But the classes came to be so much more than I'd anticipated. I was inspired not only through your exercise but also through your story. You went through a miscarriage, were diagnosed with the breast cancer, got out of a bad marriage, and remained positive. I also enjoyed the fellowship with the other ladies. All of these things motivated me to start my own aerobics business. I thought it would be a great way to help the ladies of the community and the members of Unity Baptist Tabernacle in Mount Vernon, New York.

I was right. The program has grown tremendously. We started off with a couple of dumbbells and mats. Now we have a lot of exercise equipment that people in the community have donated because they want to support the program and see the results of the participants. People can't believe the transformations. One husband came to see the class for himself because he didn't believe his wife was actually happy about going to an exercise class every Friday night. There was another woman who initially had trouble walking, but after a few sessions she was actually riding her bicycle to class. Another, who used to come to class regularly, called to tell me she had to stop because she needed to support her husband through treatment after he'd been diagnosed with cancer. After he passed away, she started coming back to class regularly but this time she brought others—her two daughters, her sister, her sister-in-law, and an aunt. It was a way for them to collectively help her through the tragedy in her life, get exercise, and be inspired to keep going every day. It gave them something to look forward to every day.

As part of the criteria for allowing people to take the aerobics class, I find out when they last saw their doctor. This forces women to look at their own health and face some of the issues they've ignored. We talk about health a lot during the classes and I do one-on-one counseling with the students following the exercise sessions. After a while, people who haven't had a physical checkup decide to go to the doctor to find out about their ailments.

Each person has their own story about what they are going through. As a result of attending the classes, three ladies underwent hysterectomies. One lady took care of a hernia problem that she'd been ignoring. Another got a breast reduction. Our biggest success story was a woman who lost thirty pounds through fasting and exercise, got a new husband, transferred down south through her job, and bought a house. She credits all of these accomplishments to my class because she believes it helped her focus on some of her dreams and goals and go after them. I'm glad to be a part of her transformation. Just recently, she sent me a card telling me that I was special and thanking me for being there when she needed me.

Currently, we have between ten and fifteen people per class. Normally, I teach the class twice a week. Exercise affects people's lives. It makes them focus on things they once ignored. Each session is ended with meditation allowing them to reflect on their day. I give them herbal tea on their way out and tell them to go home and take time for themselves. These are things they could do on their own. But the class forces them to take time out for themselves.

There's no denying that the class has tremendously helped others. But it's been a blessing to me as well. More good things have come out of this exercise program than I could have ever imagined. I've been able to donate a portion of the proceeds from the class back to the church to help them with their other projects. I've grown closer to my husband because the class is an activity that we do together. Although he's not an aerobics teacher, he's there to help me with the equipment, provide some of the ladies with male *insight, and sympathize with them because, at one time, he too was overweight. The people at the church were so impressed with my work that they invited me to do a full-fledged empowerment program for them and I got rave reviews. Furthermore, the meditation and regular exercise helped me have a great pregnancy and peace of mind and to stay centered and calm. The energy I get from the ladies helps me to prioritize my life and health. This was especially important in light of my very stressful job. I am a senior project manager for a major communications firm. I have ten project managers that report to me and we were involved in a number of high-profile projects like restoring telephone services during the 9/11 tragedy. Exercise helps me deal with the stress that I deal with every day, realize that I can still make a difference in other people's lives and put everything in perspective.*

Perhaps the biggest lesson I've learned from the experience is that the more you take care of yourself, the more you can do for others. Now, every day I try to share my gifts with others. I feel I have a very privileged life, and exercise helps me give back to the community and myself.

Are you ready to start your workout? Of course you are. Use these tips to get with an exercise program:

- Get a "good bill of health" from your physician and start out at a pace that you're comfortable with.

- Don't wait for motivation. You may never *feel* like exercising if you wait around for the notion. Instead, start exercising whether you want to or not. You need to exercise to preserve your physical and mental health so nothing should prevent you from doing it. Push yourself. Sometimes you have to act first and the inspiration and excitement will follow.

- Upgrade your walking by visiting place such as the park, the mall (just window shop), and other attractions in your city.

- Exercise in a group. Find others who share your interests so that you'll continue to be motivated on days when you don't feel like exercising. Find a class that totally meets your needs. You may not want a class with fifty students; you may only want a class with five.

- Exercise in an atmosphere that you enjoy. There have been times when I have exercised with women who don't look like me or who don't share my common weight goals or the music just isn't slammin', and before the class starts I'm in the back of the room because the atmosphere isn't conducive to my spirit. If this happens to you, find another class.

- Diversify your exercise program. Try yoga, spinning, step aerobics, and other activities. You may need a class that challenges your muscles like an aero-band class or Pilates. Find a program that enables you to work on your stomach because that's where you house your anger, resentment, and fear. An ab class challenged what I held inside. But I also needed a butt-busting class because I got a big old butt and I was always ashamed of it: This class helped me appreciate my physical beauty.

- Take a deep breath. One of the things I learned about surviving tragedy is the importance of taking time out to breathe. This allowed me to exude the feelings that I unconditionally had learned to hold in. Even though I was an aerobics instructor it took some time for me to realize that the proper breathing helps alleviate stress. It wasn't until I went through tragedy that I realized that if I hold in the feelings they make me tired, resentful, and moody.

Here are some mini-exercises that you can try to relieve stress and boost your mood:

STRETCH. When you get out of bed, stretch, by raising your hands over your head and allowing your arms to come down slowly to the left and right side of your body. Repeat this ten times.

LUNGE. Step out on your left foot and stretch the back leg; stay in that position for ten seconds. Then, do the same exercise for your right leg.

NECK STRETCH. Slowly tilt your head from the left to the right shoulder five times.

BREATHE DEEPLY. Bend your knees, shoulders back and breathe air into your stomach and slowly let the air out of your mouth. Repeat this five times.

EMOTIONAL EXERCISES FOR COPING

Exercising is not only for your physical well-being but for your mental health as well. During times of trouble, I find I need to exercise my emotions as well as my body. I do this by participating in things that I've never done before like hiking, running in a marathon, or just playing touch football with the neighborhood kids in the snow. These challenges make me feel like I'm being all that I can be and help me feel like my own private star. Despite the circumstances, exercising my emotions proves that I can still feel good about myself as well as what I can accomplish.

Try exercising your emotions for a spiritual boost. Maybe you should attend a physical healing retreat. That's what I did when I visited Akieley, an organization that sponsors retreats for women of color. It is phenomenal. My first experience at this retreat blew my mind. It's not often you see about 300 sisters gathered together for emotional and physical healing—but, more importantly, sisters embracing each other's pain and applauding one another's successes. The first night each person had to come to the front of the room to do something they'd always wanted to do but didn't have the nerve to do. I sang a song while others read poems, expressed angry or hurt feelings, danced, or just let go. We lost our fears and then we could connect to the root of our problems so we could get the most out the retreat. Then we meditated together, and the next morning everyone remained silent until we came together for a group meeting. It was so cleansing. I can go on and on. This type of experience allowed me to be myself among people that I didn't know, who didn't judge me. If a retreat isn't for you, perhaps you should try something as simple as looking in the mirror every morning and giving yourself a compliment. You'll find that you'll begin to live up to those expectations that you set up each day. For example, if you start your day by telling yourself that you have a great smile, then you'll want to smile all day long.

Speaking of smiling, try to show those pearly whites as much as you can. Now I know you might not think it's appropriate to smile during times of tribulation, and you may be right. But if you find an opportunity to smile and even laugh, snatch it up. What will happen is that your emotions will start to live up to what your body is doing. Singer Erykah Badu, in an interview with *Heart & Soul* magazine (October 2003), said it best: "If a song or a relationship doesn't turn out the way I want, first I pretend to be happy and eventually my soul catches on." She was on to something when she made this revelation. Putting your best on the outside even if you're dying on the inside does as much for you as it does for other people.

While we're talking about being at our best, let's ditch the negative thoughts. There is no place for them if you truly want to heal. Initially, when I was diagnosed with cancer I thought, "Maybe I am going to die." Or "Maybe with all the mistakes that I've made God has finally realized that he better kill me off now before I infect someone else with my negativity." When I made the decision to live, I realized that I had to kill those thoughts. I started combating them by doing a lot of praying and meditating, knowing that God resides within. I also eliminated anything that would put me in a slump so I stopped watching the news before I went to sleep at night and I eliminated any television programs containing violence or that used women as sex objects. I waved bye-bye to any shows that even hinted at pornography, and in some cases that included the latest music videos. I did all of this to help me appreciate my self-worth. As far as I was concerned I valued myself way too much to keep any negativity in space. And just like Badu promised in her interview, my soul caught on.

One more thing about emotional exercises, start practicing what you speak. In other words, choose the language you use very carefully because your words have creative power. So if you speak negativity, it will start to manifest in your life. By the same token, if you stick to positive talk, good things are sure to follow. Just ask Debrena Jackson Gandy. In her book *All the Joy You Can Stand,* she asks readers to understand the importance of what they say. "You can wreak serious havoc in your life when you don't recognize and understand the power of your spoken words," she writes. "Your words are far more than strings of syllables, nouns, verbs, and adjectives. . . . Our words convey how we see, perceive, interpret, and experience life. Thus they act as a bridge between our inner world and our outer world." She advises people to take notice of the words they use, particularly in the conversations and interactions they have with others. In her case, she started changing negative words in her vocabulary for more positive ones. For example, she has substituted "My cash flow is low" for the phrase "I'm broke." Or instead of referring to herself as "busy," she says she is "making things happen." Her "problems" have now become her "challenges." And instead of being on a diet she refers to herself as "making conscious eating choices."

Now it's your turn. Get a blank piece of paper and divide it into two columns. On one side, write down the various "negative" words or statements that you've allowed to penetrate your life. On the other side, write words or phrases that you can use as substitutes. Now commit to actually changing the words you use so you can speak positive results into your reality. You'll wish you'd acted sooner.

AND THE BOTTOM LINE IS . . .

So what does a chapter on exercise have to do with overcoming a challenge? For one thing, if you feel better physically, you're more likely to take on a more positive frame of mind. You'll be more apt to focus on the solutions rather than the problems. Also, overcoming your physical limitations will help you face, and eventually triumph, over mental challenges. In addition, your physical exercises will inspire others around you and once they upgrade their physical health, they will think better and could become a more helpful resource to you. Beyond that, the emotional exercises you implement will help you promote positive thinking and healthy talk so you can speak an optimistic future into existence.

Step 6

Accept Your Shortcomings

Shellie after her hair fell out from chemo

2/6/00

It's way too soon! I'm only three months into the pregnancy and my baby is trying to make it into the world. I'm having complications and fearing for my life. Maybe I made a mistake getting pregnant again? I'm a cancer survivor—what was I thinking? Not only did I put my life in danger but I've endangered the life of my child—how selfish, how ignorant. If my baby dies, it's all my fault.

You know I hear what the doctors are saying, but somehow I just don't believe that God would do this to me—again. I don't think God would allow me to get cancer, get pregnant, and then take the child away from me. I don't think I deserve that much pain. Also, I'm a different person now; I'm a different woman now.

In the past, I pushed God aside and decided to live in constant fear. I doubted the power of God. I stopped praying and started believing that I was in control of my destiny. It was all about me and only me.

Actually my fear also prevented me from believing in myself and my right to have a child. I didn't think I had the right to be married or be a mother. I let fear overcome me. And I know that fear has been my biggest shortcoming. Although, I can't say that I never get afraid, I certainly don't let fear rule me. Instead I trust God.

So right here, right now, I'm going to trust God again. This experience may be a setback but my baby is going to be healthy—I just know it! When you let God lead, everything else follows, and I'm so glad I'm letting him take the driver's seat.

My diagnosis of cancer put my shortcomings in full view. Throughout the whole ordeal (and even prior to getting the diagnosis), I was angry, afraid, confused, upset, and helpless at times. And that was okay. I allowed myself to feel each and every one of those emotions, I just didn't allow myself to obsess over them. I realized early on that everything that I was feeling and everything that I was going through was in the divine order. My responses allowed me to put things into perspective. Later, I used that same energy to discover the reasons why I was alive in the first place and further explored the changes I had left to do. Since I'd convinced myself that there was more work to do, my future became more attractive and I looked forward to being around to see it.

Had cancer never come into my life, I would never have recognized that there was anything wrong with me. Cancer also helped me realize that there is something wrong with everyone. Not one person on this earth is perfect. Yet, we as black women often feel that we have to be twice as good and work twice as hard to be acknowledged as simply adequate. As difficult as that can be, focusing on it won't get you anywhere when you're trying to overcome a challenge. In fact, you need to abandon any notions you have about being perfect. The fact is: Your actions won't always be perfect and you may not live up to other people's standards. Your decisions, though far from perfect, are based on what you've experienced and that's part of life. Your choices—right or wrong—are the ones that you are responsible for and you can't beat yourself up about the outcome.

Take me, for example. At one time I was a procrastinator, but when I started enduring life's trials, I was forced to take action because it didn't appear I had a lot of time left to waste. But I shouldn't have waited until I was faced with a terminal illness to come to that conclusion and neither should you. "We all procrastinate to a point but not to the point of doing nothing. But you don't procrastinate nearly as much now," my mom counters proudly. "I'm not saying you're perfect, but at least you recognize that you have shortcomings and try to deal with them. Some people have shortcomings and they don't want people to tell them about it. And then there are those of us that only admit the shortcomings to ourselves. But when you are confronted with those shortcomings you need to address them, not hide from them."

Besides you really can't hide from them, you only think you can. Every step that you take and every challenge that you face is all a part of your work in progress. Even your shortcomings are part of the divine plan for your life. Don't fear the experience you're going through, because God's will is working itself out day by day. And whether you believe it or not, your faults and/or shortcomings make you unique and will contribute to the ultimate outcome in your life.

This again became apparent to me the other day. I made a speech to a group of young kids graduating from a program at the YWCA. I encouraged them to let go of ill feelings because those bad feelings can turn into disease and they run the risk of experiencing just what I did. I received a standing ovation. I put my entire life out there. I told them about my cancer treatment and there was a sense of freedom. If you keep your experiences to yourself, then you're only living for you. But if you share yourself, then you are the one that gets the gift. So I tell the truth, all truths. I let people know how bad Shellie *was* so they can use my story as an opportunity to reexamine their own lives.

Typically, things that break us—a broken spirit, a broken heart— tend to make us gravitate toward those people we see as living a successful life. Just remember that those are their successes—not yours. Accepting your own shortcomings allows you to seek the individual from within for answers and develop expectations for yourself. We begin to live life for us through us. And that's what we're supposed to do anyway.

Sometimes your shortcomings were given to you because God knew who you would become. For instance, the disease forced me to recognize the resentment or the pain I'd experienced. Now I can use those same experiences to inspire others because I can personally relate to their feelings of anger, resentment, bitterness, and fear. My shortcomings became the forces that inspired me to make a change and deal with the issues that were holding me back. Some people go through their whole lives without ever knowing why they are who they are. I now know. This has allowed me to motivate so many others to break the bonds that prevent them from reaching their potential.

So how can you use your shortcomings as an opportunity to grow and bring yourself to a better awareness of what tomorrow may bring? We'll look at how you can identify your shortcomings, compensate for them, use them to your advantage, and select the best solutions for the situation that you're in despite your shortcomings. I hope you'll come to the same conclusion that I did: All things work together for good—they really do.

FROM WRONG TO RIGHT

As crazy as it sounds, I didn't know that I had any character defects until I was given a death sentence. Even when I lost a child, I still didn't re-assess my life and gain a greater appreciation for the things I should have valued. As a result, the universe had to do something on an even larger scale to get my attention. I hope you realize how your inability to honestly assess your shortcomings can contribute to the calamities that occur in your life. Pay attention today, so you don't find yourself in an even worse situation in the future.

Remember, I am writing this book in hopes that you don't make the same mistakes that I did. I hope you'll understand my pain and consider me your sacrificial lamb. Use my suffering as your chance to live a more fruitful and emotionally stable life by learning to take an honest look at yourself and making a commitment to change for the better.

Usually we never see what's wrong with us until others bring it to our attention or until we are faced with tragedy. Use this time to access your feelings and pick out those negative actions and thoughts. Assess the things that keep you from thinking positively about yourself and from living life to the absolute fullest. Do you use too much foul language? Do you gossip? Do you steal from others both emotionally and physically? Are you promiscuous? Are you envious? Are you a liar? Are you controlling? Sit in a quiet room and listen to your spirit so you can evaluate your existence and the people you have in your life. Write those shortcomings down. Then, grab hold of that which makes you feel good and beautiful to God and yourself.

Once you realize your shortcomings, I advise you to just flip the script. Get in the habit of doing the opposite of whatever behavior is getting in your way. For instance, if you are an impatient person, simply be patient. You may struggle at first, but if you truly want to get to the next level in your life, if you're committed to overcoming this particular problem, then you also have to be committed to purging yourself of anything that's poisoning your system, including your own behavior. Make that change.

You're probably saying to yourself, change really isn't that easy—particularly if you've had a particular shortcoming that has taken hold of your life for years. But change *is* easy. Experts say you need to do something at least twenty-one days before it's officially a habit (or before you officially break a habit). I don't know if that's true or not. I think it depends on the individual. But I do know, if you are serious about making a change then you can "just do it" (yes, I've borrowed a slogan from Nike because those sneaker makers are on to something). I'll prove it to you. When your house is burning down, nobody has to tell you to get the hell out, you just do it. Even if you've never been in a fire before, something in your brain tells you that you and your family are in danger and you do what you need to do to save yourself. Well I'm telling you that your house is on fire and unless you do something to rescue yourself, you are in danger of allowing this last blow to knock you completely out of the game of life. Don't wait for the motivation to change, it may never come. Just like I told you about exercise, you don't really need motivation to start participating in a particular activity—sometimes you have to do the work first and the inspiration will follow.

MAKING A LIST AND CHECKING IT TWICE

Do you have your list complete, yet? It's okay if you don't because it's a list that will change throughout the course of your life—maybe even day by day or moment by moment. You may need to get some help from other people around you. Ask them to honestly tell if there is anything about you that needs to be improved or changed? Of course, you need to take what they say with a grain of salt because some people are not responding to what you need to change but to what they feel uncomfortable with. A friend might tell you that you talk too much because he or she is having problems holding up their end of the conversation. At the same time, if you keep hearing the same types of things from different people, (let's say three people use the word "controlling" to describe you) then maybe you should consider adding it to your list.

As for me, there have been several times in my life when I have allowed my resentment to hold me back from some of the greatest opportunities I had to make a difference in my life and others. I didn't communicate with someone about something important because I was still holding on to some past stuff. That's not fair to them or me. I also allowed fear to take root in my life. That was an awful trick that I played on myself because I allowed the emotion to prevent me from living up to my true potential. Now whenever something in my head tells me that I can't do something, I see it for the lie that it is and tell myself that "I can." I tell myself that I can do all things through Christ that strengthen me and the fear dissipates.

But resentment and fear were just two of the things on my list. People have also told me that I eat too much, gossip, am impatient, fear not being liked, am too independent, indulge in too much junk food, have a tendency to make little things harder than they need to be, am insecure, and lack confidence. Now, I wasn't comfortable hearing those things but I needed to hear them if I was going to improve my life. You need to hear them too. So start polling the people who know you best so you can start to be your best.

KEEPING IT REAL IN THE MIDST OF CHALLENGE

You remember how Janice Lee showed us how she maintained an attitude of gratitude as she was going through her string of challenges. For instance, instead of being angry about her brother's long-term illness, she looked at it as an opportunity for her to make amends with him before his death. Here she provides more helpful advice by suggesting ways to identify your limitations so you can get the help you need to overcome a challenge.

- Surround yourself with a group of people who will love you enough to be honest with you. During a tragedy you want people in your life who will tell you those things you *need* to hear rather than stick to things you want to hear. They just might have the critical information you need to save your life. Don't be afraid to be pushed beyond your comfort zone. The people who push you probably see your potential more clearly than you do, and they are actually helping you grow. Trust that they see the personal barriers that may be keeping you from realizing your greatest possibilities. I depend on my "sister-spirits" for this type of support. As far as I'm concerned, they are women who are close enough to be blood sisters and are an integral part of my life. I can depend on them to be there no matter what and to give it to me straight.

- Look to your family for strength. Even when you have challenging relationships within your family, know that these people are often hidden treasures whom you can depend on for support. For example, my source of strength comes from the lessons I've learned from my parents, particularly as it relates to their migration to New York from the south. They demonstrated tenacity when they became the first African-American family to integrate a white community in the Bronx. I witnessed my father's passion for learning as I watched him educate himself by tapping various resources. I learned to respect and honor my mother's continuous struggle to keep our family together. Please don't let your current crisis and conflict within your family blind you from the blessings they provide. They have a valuable story to share, and there are lessons we can learn from their lives.

- Learn to love others for who they are and not for what you wish for them to be. You can't change other people, so just stop trying to do so. Why would you want to change them anyway? They are God's divine invention. Instead, think of ways you can nurture the relationship that you have with them, regardless of the faults we all have (yes, you have them too!).

- Recognize that you are just one peg in the wheel. Learn to let go and let God. We each play a role in His master plan, so work at fulfilling your role and allow God to help others fill theirs. I am learning that change begins with me. No matter how "right" I might be, I bring my own dynamic to the crisis. I may not be able to control a crisis or other people's actions but I can control my responses and my attitude. As I take steps in self-improvement, I see that others follow suit!

- Learn to trust your inner spirit. When your soul speaks, take time to listen. Nurture that "voice" within you and allow yourself to use it as your guide throughout your life.

- Acknowledge the little girl within you. Do you sometimes feel like the little child in a big person's body? Don't worry, we all feel that way at times. But, just because we feel that way that doesn't mean we can't love the little girl in us and allow her to interact with others. God keeps her safe. But it's up to you to allow her to be free to love, make mistakes, dream, and trust.

USING WHAT YOU'VE GOT TO GET THINGS DONE

Remember we said that all things work together for good—even when it comes to your shortcomings. That was the truth, sis. Most of the time, our shortcomings can block God's blessings and keep us from operating at our best. But there are some times when we need those faults (for lack of a better word) because they are a part of our protective mechanisms. While fear is never a good thing to have if it paralyzes you, it is very useful if it causes you to seek a second or third opinion in a medical crisis. You just need to know when that shortcoming that you put away might be helpful to you. Just put it back in the safe when you're finished using it.

As I've told you, I realize that my impatience can be interpreted as a shortcoming. But at times I have used this shortcoming to my advantage because my impatience has inspired me to get things done or given me the courage to step up to the head of a situation to get things moving. As another example, my talking too much has helped me land lots of speaking engagements.

There have even been instances when my anger has enabled me to acquire important information. I remember one time when I was at an African-American Women's Health summit in a room with a host of women and one male doctor who was discussing the cures for breast cancer. The women on the panel were running down statistics about the prevalence of breast cancer, but as far as I was concerned they weren't discussing the real problem: How do we get African-American women to change their minds about living? As they continued their presentations, I was getting angrier and angrier until I finally stood up with tears in my eyes. I said, "Ladies I am a breast cancer survivor that was diagnosed at age twenty-nine, and we are not talking about the real issues that involve breast cancer. I think we should be talking about what we can do to alleviate stress, address single parent issues, tackle our insecurities, deal with our unforgiveness, and look at those things that prevent us from valuing ourselves so that we'll be inspired to get regular examinations." Other women in the audience agreed. Then the doctor countered by saying we need to focus on the cancer. I stood up again and disagreed with his theory. After I spoke, I had a line of women waiting to discuss my issues—things that they were also trying to overcome. I will never forget that experience. If my anger hadn't inspired me to take a stand, the women in that audience would never have heard another opinion and may not have ever had their issues addressed.

I also remember being at an exclusive club in Manhattan. The audience was filled with white women discussing new findings regarding breast cancer. After sitting there and listening to all the new advances in the area of breast cancer I was amazed and felt left behind. My anger kicked in. When they opened up the floor for questions, I asked "What do I do now to get these new advances? Should I get my entire medical records reassessed?" I got applause for my question, and that led to lots of other questions. It seemed that people were too intimidated to speak their minds but my anger made me brave. For me, when I use my anger in the right context, it has helped me get the answers I need to stay healthy.

And then there are things that could be viewed as shortcomings at first that may become your asset. For example, I am a full-figured woman and I've always looked at that as a shortcoming. But once I started teaching aerobics, my hefty size inspired a lot of people to exercise because they stopped buying into the myth that heavyset people can't be physically fit—they absolutely can be and I'm living proof. Your size shouldn't control your destiny.

GETTING READY FOR A COMEBACK

You've heard the adage that whatever you do comes back to you. Well, you better believe it, sis. Let me point to something that happened on a job to show you how this works. I remember working in a not-for-profit agency to help people get their films done. It was an excellent organization with a good reputation. I got the job as program manager. I was so excited. Finally, my first big movie job. Well I worked from 9 A.M. to 10 P.M. most nights. The organization couldn't afford to have a lot of people working for them. From the first day, the business manager had it in for me. I tried several times to reach out, but to no avail. Then the company hired a new executive director who was very nice. The business manager made it her business to make friends with the new head honcho. One week after our new boss took her post, she fired me. I was so upset. She had no grounds for firing me, I was doing a great job. I remember walking the streets of Manhattan with tears in my eyes. I walked from downtown to midtown. I told all of my friends what happened. They convinced me that it was the agency's loss. Three months later, the organization folded. Six months later, a friend of mine, a head hunter, called me at my new job and asked me if I knew someone he was considering for a position. It was the executive director who fired me. He asked me if she was the lady that fired me for no apparent reason. I told him "Yes." She didn't get the position. That confirmed what I'd always believed: What goes around comes around.

But perhaps you thought the term "comeback" for the opening of this section was going to discuss ways that you can "come back" after you eliminate or at least greatly reduce the presence of your shortcomings. You were right. Once you get rid of the garbage, you can feel secure in knowing that those things no longer take hold of your life. That's powerful. Now you have the ability to make decisions based on the facts that exist, not the things that were once colored by your own limitations. You deserve that kind of freedom. So take hold of it and celebrate the new you, knowing that God has given you all that you need to get where you need to go.

BEING A WORK IN PROGRESS

I'm better than I was yesterday but I'll be even better tomorrow. I do realize, however, that perfection is a lifelong journey, not a destination. So every once in a while, I eat things that are not good for me because I'm still trying to overcome my love of certain foods. As a breast cancer survivor, I should always try to be as healthy as possible, particularly since research suggests that obesity has been linked to cancer. I have this information and strive to consistently maintain a diet and exercise program that will support my recovery. But there are times I fall short. I don't beat myself up about it. I take responsibility for it. In May 2003, when I attended a writing workshop, I did exactly that. The facilitator requested that the participants write letters to ourselves. Here is what I came up with:

Dear Shellie:
You don't know your body very well. You have caused it a lot of grief because of accidents and near death experiences. Now, I want you to take your time and love yourself. I want you to learn to love your body with the same tenacity that you use to love your husband. I want you to dive deeply into learning who you are just as you are learning to know who God is. Continue to pray because that is your link to understanding yourself.

Continue to exercise because it will give you the energy you need to take better care of yourself and others. It will also allow you to fall in love with yourself and the God within you. And stop watching so much television. Instead, read more and love your

*family more. Continue to do, give, embrace, relax, and live your
life to your fullest.*

*Stop running from success. As long as you are giving your life
up for God, then you must know that success is your divine right.
With that said, make sure you don't put anything ahead of God.
For example, don't let the love of money or the love of anything
else get in the way of fulfilling God's purpose for your life. You
can't enjoy a harmonious life or loving spirit if you allow the
enemy to control you. So stop the devil in his tracks.*

*Now, here's your new declaration: I want to be graceful. I
want to exercise daily. I want to eat healthy. I want to nourish the
God inside of me who wants me to serve the universe. I want
peace. I want joy, happiness, and wealth. I want to get rid of the
love handles that now cling to my waist. I want to trust myself
and, more importantly, trust God to guide my life. I am releasing
self in order to be guided by God's spirit. I want to continuously
thank God for allowing me to be a good mother and wife. I want
to continuously show gratitude to God for blessing me with my
husband and son. I am going to be guided by God in everything
I do.*

On a regular basis, I take responsibility for my shortcomings,
reaffirm my commitment to make the necessary changes for self-
improvement and continue to take steps to achieve my goals. If I mess
up, I wash the slate clean and start again. You can do the same. The
good thing about life is that as long as you live you have the ability to
design a new life—breath by breath and moment by moment. So start
designing a life that you love today.

Step 7

Dream On . . .

Shellie married Abdeltif Tazi on November 27, 1999.

8/10/01

Today is Monday. It's not only the beginning of the work week, it's also the start of some questions that I have been having lately. Mainly, why do I have to make a difference? Sometimes I just want to come home, relax, and take care of me and my family. Why must I be a catalyst for change? That's such a hard job. I guess this idea is especially fresh in my head because I'm coming home from my aerobics class and I am tired—downright exhausted. Probably, because I am doing too much. I am still full-figured and I sometimes wonder if I will ever reach my personal weight goal. I am sweaty and wonder if I am going to stop teaching.

Just a moment ago, the phone rang. I was reluctant to answer it, particularly since I had just told my husband that I am going to stop teaching aerobics. He told me to do what I wanted. Sometimes I don't know what I want. At times, I don't think it's totally my choice. When I answered the phone, I was surprised to find it was Monique Brown from Professional Women of Color. It was 8:45 P.M. and I had no idea why she was calling. She proceeded to ask me what I had been doing since the last time we spoke. I told her that I was teaching aerobics, raising my family, and working full-time. She asked me if I had ever been approached about writing my story. Her book, It's a Sistah Thing: A Guide to Understanding and Dealing with Fibroids for Black Women, *is coming out this year and she wants to start working on another project. She says she was so impressed by my speaking appearances that I was her first consideration. According-ing to her, she has an awesome agent that she would love for me to meet with to see if it's possible to get a publisher interested in my story. Monique really put the fire under my butt. And I just knew this project was going to turn out to be a great opportunity and it is. Berkley Books loved the idea and the rest is history. Now I realize I have to keep teaching aerobics and I have to share my story with the world because I'm not living my life for me. The lessons I've learned from my life's challenges weren't just my lessons. They were lessons for all of us, to show us that no matter how bad things get, there is al-ways room for dreams. So now I know that no matter what things come my way, I'll never stop planning for tomorrow. I continue to dream and know they'll come true.*

By far, this was my toughest chapter to write. For some reason, I found it challenging to tell people the importance of dreaming when they are in the midst of a storm. Then it hit me: I'm not telling people to continue dreaming because that's something that they want to do. I'm telling people to dream because that's what they have to do. You have to be able to dream if you are ever going to overcome tough times.

My dad really brings the point home when he talks about his dreams. Even though he endured an illness that has kept him in and out of the hospital for half of his life, he still dreams and is even optimistic. "I know God holds my future, but I would love to see my ten grandchildren grow up to be young men and women." And he says this with great anticipation, as if he expects this dream to come to pass. "I'd like to see them grow up so I can see how the Lord has blessed them. I'd love to see them run, play, and entertain. I also look forward to getting another transplant, knowing that I'm going to get the transplant when God is ready for me to have it."

Psychologist Julia Boyd believes that "dreaming is the most important thing we can do." According to Boyd, it's part of our survival instinct. "It's only when we stop dreaming that we admit defeat," she insists, noting that most people who experience success dream about their accomplishments before they are ever realized. When tragedy strikes, it's important that we hold on to our ability to dream of a better tomorrow, because that's the first step to making things happen. Now you may go in and out of a state of optimism and dip into despair, but you still need to dream—maybe it's for a cure, how beautiful heaven will be, what great lives your children will have, or even for a better world overall. "If anybody picks up this book I hope they learn that nothing should stand in the way of them having a dream," adds Boyd.

I dream constantly, especially after I was diagnosed with breast cancer. On the day that I was diagnosed and my ex-husband left me, my biggest fear was that I would die alone. So I got on my knees and asked God to send me people who would love me the same way that he did and I conjured up visions of that possibility. The results exceeded my expectations. People who didn't know me came out of the woodwork to lend a helping hand. Only a few months following what I thought was the worst day of my life, I met my new prince.

When I saw my second husband for the first time I believed I saw an angel. He actually had a light around his face. It was during my first three months of chemo when I was teaching an aerobics class at the YWCA. He worked at the facility and we became fast friends. I asked him where he was from he told me to guess. "It has to be Italy or Puerto Rico," I answered. "You can't be Dominican." He smiled when he told me that he was actually from Morocco. Hmmm, that sounded interesting but I didn't even know where that was on the globe. "It's in North Africa," he explained. His gentle, kind spirit was incredibly intoxicating. From what I could tell, he seemed to have a real appreciation for people and the love he expressed was uncondi-tional. I'd never met a man like that and I began to appreciate all of the love that he continued to show me. He and I did everything to-gether, and he was always there to help me. Our bond grew. I fell in love with him almost instantly, and when I called my friend Jennifer to tell her the news she reminded me about my old ways. "Girl, you are breaking all of the rules," she teased. But that was okay because I was opening up myself to new possibilities.

Talk of marriage soon followed. We were at Edgars Café on the Upper West Side. I had my list of all of the reasons why I couldn't get married; I might die soon; my last husband left me; I'm too dam-aged; I'm bald (at that time he didn't even know I had to wear a wig because of hair loss from chemo); and worst of all the cancer treat-ments will probably prevent me from having children. As fast as I blurted out the excuses, he knocked them down. He wanted us to cherish the time that we had left—"no matter how long that turns out to be," he said gently. As far as children were concerned, he looked at me and told me that if we could have children then we'd have something to take care of for the rest of our lives. But if we couldn't, that would give us an opportunity to travel the world together for the rest of our days. "We aren't going to start acting like the people on soap operas, declaring, 'Oh my God, my life is over because we can't have children,'" he insisted. When he said that, tears started rolling down my face because I had no more excuses and was ready to move forward.

We got engaged, pregnant, and then married (yes, that was the order) shortly after. It was the happiest time of my life. I married my Prince Charming. Now that is not to say that he's perfect, just perfect for me and I thank God daily for His gift. Another gift followed closely on the heels of our marriage: our son, Amir Abdeltif Tazi, was born on May 17, 2000, at ten pounds, two ounces without a blemish.

Sis, I don't care how bad things look; you need to know that there is always something better for you waiting on the other side. But you have to truly believe that in your heart. I am a witness that the Creator will give you everything you've ever lost as long as you keep the faith (and remember your faith only has to be the size of a mustard seed, according to the Bible). Now I'm able to take those stumbling blocks in my life and turn them into stepping stones so I can write this book. Who would have thought?

I am one of so many people who had to force themselves to dream in the face of adversity. So you're not alone. In fact, everybody you know who has actually made it through hard times has had to hold onto their dreams as they journeyed on a troubled road to their heart's desire. To triumph is never easy but that is, after all, why it is so rare and highly valued. Trust me, sis, God gives you everything you need to travel the road ahead. I remember wishing that my life was easier or that I could be somebody else. But now, as I look back, I wouldn't have traded my size twelve shoes for any others. I am on an extraordinary assignment, and the lessons that come from my experiences are designed especially for me.

For everything in life, there is a reason and a season. At one time, I didn't believe that, but now I know that to be true. Things don't just happen. We help them happen by what we think, feel, speak, and dream. Prior to my bout with breast cancer and divorce, I had tunnel vision and couldn't view the world beyond what I could physically see. But once I was told I was going to die and my ex-husband abandoned me, I was forced to either die or live and dream up a better tomorrow.

At one time, I'd just consider things that I wanted without any real thought to how I'd make those things a reality. Years before being diagnosed with breast cancer, I wrote down a long list of the things that I wanted to achieve in my lifetime, they included becoming a talk show host, being popular, owning a mansion, having two children, and being the envy of all of my friends. Sounds trite? Maybe, but at least I had a clear sense of the things that were important to me at that time, and that's important if you want to conquer any calamity. You need dreams—ones that are so big and insane that you're probably too afraid to share them with anyone. Your dreams should be bigger than anything you could ever fathom because you'll be that much more impressed when God makes them come to pass. You need dreams because they signify hope, an essential belief required for your survival.

This chapter will compel you to look at your own life's plan and develop strategies to realize your dreams. Now if you've already accepted your current situation as a death sentence, then this chapter isn't for you. In order to be able to dream, you have to believe you'll be around (even in the supernatural) to enjoy them when they manifest.

But on the other hand, if you are willing to leap into the unknown and dare the ridiculous, this chapter will help you chart out a course. And if you don't feel inspired to dream, I challenge you to do it anyway. I truly didn't believe that I was destined for greatness but now it's at my doorstep on a daily basis. What the enemy meant for bad, God meant for good. My future continues and so do my dreams.

JOEL 2:28

And afterward, I will pour out my Spirit on all people. Your sons and daughters will prophesy, your old men will dream dreams, your young men will see visions.

SUCCESS BREEDS SUCCESS

Sis, you've heard the saying that birds of a feather flock together. Well, the same thing goes for people who overcome tragedy. If you keep company with overcomers, some of their magic will rub off on you. Take my friend Jakki Taylor as an example. I don't care what's going on, this sister always manages to do her thing. That was a good lesson for me because I started believing in things that I once thought were impossible as I witnessed her successes. I needed to see her life. When I met Jakki, she was a producer for ABC TV, which was my ideal job. Girlfriend was happy, slim, educated, high-spirited, and handling her business as a powerful executive. It's not that she didn't have bad things happen to her, she absolutely did, but she never lost sight of her will to be more than what she was. Plus, her love for God kept her strong and fearless.

But here's how keeping Jakki's company (and her success) worked wonders for me. Jakki was working for ABC's *The View* when I got the opportunity to be a guest. When I arrived at the studio she was there to give me support. Right before it was my turn to be on the air, I admitted to Jakki that I was afraid because I realized how important this opportunity was to share my message about breast cancer and fitness. Jakki pulled me in the bathroom and suggested that we pray together. We prayed and I thanked God for having Jakki as a good friend and we both thanked God for putting us in the position to change the hearts and minds of his people. We also asked God to continue to use us for good and to help us both live out our dreams. Now

Jakki is working for the number-one show in the country. And by now, you know everything that has happed to me, including marriage, motherhood, and this book deal. And just think: God is not even finished with us yet.

In *The Game: Win Your Life in 90 Days,* author Sarano Kelley classifies relationships in four categories: (A) relationships that restore and nurture you by holding you to a high standard and expecting you to fulfill your life's purpose (e.g., clergyman, personal coach, some family and friends); (B) relationships that just help you maintain the status quo (unfortunately family members often fall into this category) by accepting your excuses for not being as great as you need to be; (C) relationships that have no real relevance in your life and may even be draining your resources (may include associates or people you don't know that well); and (D) relationships that bring out the worst in you because people in this category allow you to gossip, whine, or ask for pity. Kelley suggests you spend most of your time nurturing "A" relationships and transforming "B" relationships into "A" relationships. These people should be your priority because they are interested (and in some instances supportive) in having you fulfill your life's purpose. As for the "C" relationships, try to spend as little time as possible with people in this category and make an effort to completely eliminate any interaction with people in the "D" category, because they bring out the worst in you. According to Kelley, this isn't about judging people: "Very fine and upstanding people can have inefficient or even hurtful relationships that bring out the worst instead of the best in each other," he writes. Looking at how you spend your time, and with whom you spend it, can help you "gain clarity on how you relate to them."

But being able to dream is not only linked to the people you hang out with. It also has to do with the activities that you're participating in. My godmother insists on keeping up with exercise even when life is tough. "Sometimes that's hard to do when you're going through a difficult time but you have to keep pushing," she says. "When I lost one of my sisters, I'd just started an exercise program at a fitness center. Initially, I would leave the exercise class feeling guilty because I was able to exercise and enjoy the class at the same time I was grieving for my sister. But I had to fight with myself and convince myself that I needed to exercise for health and stress relief. It's important to recognize that you need to do something to have fun. Not that you have forgotten the bad situation, but you've pushed it out of your mind to allow you to indulge in your own life. It's called survival. I had to think about all of the things I needed to do to help me survive. And the first thing I needed to do was take care of myself."

Kelley has also designed a rating system to assess the things you do on a daily basis. He says there are activities that: (A) nourish you, which would include prayer, meditation, exercise, spending time with your family, recording your thoughts in a journal, or reading a bedtime story to your kids; (B) stress you out because you only participate in them in response to an emergency, such as if your doctor calls to warn you about your health, you might increase your exercise, stop smoking, or change your diet—things you should have been doing all along; (C) undervalue you because these are things that could be done by someone else, like the laundry, housecleaning, or cleaning out your filing cabinet; and (D) drain you because these activities have absolutely no benefit, they include things like gossiping, criticizing, backbiting, or just stirring up trouble. According to Kelley, participating in "B, C, and D activities prevent you from fulfilling your life goals." He says your ultimate goals should be to "spend the majority of your day doing A activities with an A relationship."

The other way success breeds success is by enabling you to get into the habit of stretching yourself. According to Boyd, each of us should offer ourselves the gift of challenge. "When we do this, we feel self-empowered. If I can climb a mountain, I can do anything!" she exclaims. "Every time you put a challenge before yourself, it forces you to do what you need to do to take that challenge on. You feel more empowered simply because you attempted it. That's the beauty."

Fortunately, I've always carried that lesson with me throughout my life. When I was in high school I was president of my class and I received the Who's Who Among High School Students in America Award. As far as I was concerned, that basically meant that I was destined to be Who's Who in everything I do throughout my life. I was committed to being in the upper echelon of society—somebody that others should know.

But I would have never had those expectations if I hadn't allowed myself to gather some achievements under my belt. The more things you attempt in life, the more things you have the opportunity to succeed at and those wins will enable you to visualize a great future. When cancer struck, I vowed to spend more time doing things that mattered. I spent more time with my family, walked across the George Washington Bridge, took a thirteen-mile hike into the mountains of New Paltz, New York, laughed more, played more, called friends and family to tell them how much I loved them, threw a thirtieth birthday bash and earned a new appreciation for my life. I also danced until my clothes were drenched and shouted at church retreats where I connected with other sisters who were also going through their own challenges. I even went to a "reach to recovery" getaway where all of us wrote down all of the things that were preventing us from being the real women we could be and then we burned those lists in a bonfire. I figure if I do things that are emotionally challenging, I'll continue to build my character and conquer my illness in the process. And if those activities weren't enough, I adopted a godmother who is sixty-seven years young. On an ongoing basis, I draw from her wisdom. All of these things, enable me to keep my dreams alive.

In addition to my character-challenging activities, I am committed to spending the rest of my days helping people discover their maximum potential. As far as I'm concerned, I was given life so I can teach others to live. I could have chosen to die but, through the grace of God, I found the strength to live and help others step into a brighter tomorrow. I don't just dream for me, I dream for others, too.

Your dreams should be a reflection of where you truly want to go. So ask yourself some questions to establish your direction: What things do you want out of your life? Is it spending more time with your family? Pursuing an entrepreneurial venture? Do you want to get married? Are children in your future? Do you want to write a book? Be honest with yourself and then make a list. Meditate on each of those things and visualize them becoming a reality. Then allow your mind, with God's lead, to start constructing a plan so you can realize your heart's desire. I implore you to take action before calamity strikes. Although it took cancer for me to more fully participate in more fulfilling activities, you shouldn't wait for that type of alarm before you start living your dreams.

BIG DREAMS, BIG RESULTS

Who cares if nobody sees what you see? It doesn't matter if you have your sights set on things that the average person can't visualize. There are some things that can't be seen with the naked eye. Be glad that you have the ability to see possibility before others do. That's what faith is: a strong belief in something that you can't physically touch. The picture will crystallize soon enough.

I wish I had not been so doubtful about my future success because now I realize that when I doubted my future, I was actually doubting God's existence in my life. I was being what the church ladies would call a "Doubting Thomas." Part of me believed God would deliver me from my troubles, but another part of me was afraid that I'd be disappointed. Then at some point, I decided that I had to trust that God wouldn't forsake me. So instead of doubting God, I prepared myself to receive all that my Creator had to offer. I learned that He wants more for his children than we want for ourselves. We can't even fathom the blessings that God wants to manifest in our lives.

At the same time, know that your ability to dream will definitely be tested. Last March, I lost a second baby due to an ectopic pregnancy. After finally being able to conceive after a year and a half, I felt like a failure. Here I was writing a book about overcoming tragedies and I was faced with another heartbreak. I finally thought my tragic life was over when I was thrown another curve. For a moment, I concluded that I needed to leave this dream stuff alone. But then I was reminded that if "God brings you to it, he'll get you through it."

That's not to say that the experience wasn't painful. At times I wanted to give up and just be like everyone else. "I've been trying to stand up for struggling sisters and look where it has gotten me," I said to myself. I wasn't sure if my dreams were worth believing in, and I was considering kicking them to the curb. And then my mother confided in me that she'd thought of me as her hero. "Shellie, ever since you were a child, you've always ended up a winner," she proclaimed. The message became clear. If we want to affect true change, we must be willing to suffer for the greater good. Everything that I was going through was intended to make a point to those people who needed to be inspired to press on. My latest loss, reaffirmed my belief that we are all here for a reason and that God in His infinite power loves us so much that He constantly gives us opportunities to learn about, as well as impact, the world around us. Contrary to what we may believe, we don't face challenges because we're weak; we face them because we are strong and need chances to help us further develop our potential. Just take a look at the earth's surface. Notice that most of the greenery is located in the valley, not on the mountaintops. So even though you experience the most pain in the valley, that's also where you experience the most growth and opportunity for reward. And that my friend is reason enough to hold on to your dreams.

So despite my hitting another low point just a few months prior to this project being completed, I didn't power down the computer just yet. Instead, I decided to include my latest tragedy in the book proving that nobody has a "free pass" when it comes to tragedy. But that still shouldn't stop you from living life to the fullest and dreaming up a world of new and improved possibilities. So dream for yourself and dream for your future.

MAKE UP YOUR MIND; THE REST WON'T MATTER

Sistahs, I'm living proof that you can change your prognosis if you change your mind. If I had internalized the medical information that was available then I would have been doomed to die—literally. One night, I came home after chemo and crumpled to the floor. I really thought that I had taken my last breath. But later, I gathered myself up and lay across my bed. From 4 P.M. that Friday evening through 9 A.M. Saturday morning, I cried. The phone rang practically all night, but I didn't answer it. Then at 9 A.M., I finally picked up my phone and heard the voice of my godmother, Marie Williams, on the other end. She told me that she had been calling all night but there was no answer. Through tears and a shivering voice I told her that I was dying and couldn't move. "What do you mean you can't move?" she cried. I told her again that I couldn't move and felt paralyzed, like I was going to die. Now my godmother, being the tough lady that she is who didn't take any crap, responded, "Shellie look outside. Do you see how bright that sun is?" I answered yes. And she continued, "When I get over there in the next fifteen minutes, I am not coming upstairs and you better have your behind downstairs at the front door waiting for me so we can go have breakfast and then do whatever."

Guess where I was in thirteen minutes. You guessed it. Me and my pitiful self were both waiting as my godmother had ordered. We headed to Borders in nearby Eastchester, then we had a bagel and juice and started browsing around the store. Without even looking where I was going, the first book I saw was an audiobook on how a woman survived breast cancer. I was amazed and started to cry. It was my signal telling me that I had to fight. It also proved to me, that sometimes your mind can enable you to do things even when your body has given up. As long as you have the mind to do something, then the rest really doesn't matter.

Challenges come in all forms but you must manage your mind, so you can impact the results.

DON'T WORRY, BE HAPPY FOR OTHER PEOPLE, TOO

I know when you're going through something tough, it might be kind of difficult to be happy for someone else. I say be happy anyway. It's important that you learn that life is not always going to be about you. It's not always going to be your turn, your reward, your accomplishment, your child, or your dream. But you have a responsibility to make other people's dreams come true, too. And a funny thing happens when you concentrate on other people: Their good fortune begins to rub off on you. It's as though you become blessed by association.

At the same time, you can also delay your blessing by being self-absorbed. We all know those sisters who are so bummed out about not being married that you can see the despair on their faces when someone in their circle ties the knot. Their "sour grapes" attitude shows up in everything they do and say. They'd rather go to the electric chair than watch another one of their girlfriends get married. And they've categorized all men as trifling, insisting that the reason their last relationship didn't work out was the other person's fault. Yet, these same women are argumentative, sarcastic, and defensive. Now I'm no relationship expert, but I'd say that's no way to get a man. Who needs that type of drama?

Perhaps they'd get better results if they stopped focusing on themselves and got involved in activities that aren't necessarily centered around *them* getting a man. Maybe if they'd asked that friend of theirs what she did to make her relationship work rather than envying her, they'd pick up some tips for themselves. Or if they just tried to be genuinely happy for somebody else, they'd actually enjoy the moment.

There's not enough room in your spirit to house your dreams *and* feelings of jealousy, envy, greed, or backbiting. These tagalongs merely prevent you from realizing the special opportunities that God has designed for your life. Don't worry about what other people are doing (or dreaming). You've got your own mission to fulfill. Instead of looking over someone else's shoulder, look up so you won't miss your own blessing.

JUST DO IT!

What would you do if you realized that your time left on earth was short? If you're anything like me, you'd make a commitment to participate in activities and spend time with people that really matter to you. But our heart's desires shouldn't be held at bay until we get to a point in our lives when we think there is no tomorrow. If you wait until then, it may be too late. Change your way of thinking while you have the chance.

Perhaps you've gotten so entrenched in the habit of delaying your happiness that you don't know how else to live. A popular R&B song declares, "I'm not your superwoman," and when it first hit the airwaves, sisters from coast to coast sang it almost as a national anthem. But despite our enthusiasm for the lyrics, we still act like superwomen because we tend to everyone else's needs at the expense of our own. When tragedy strikes, we think that's even more of a reason to ignore our own feelings. Instead, we focus on the concerns of our parents, kids, siblings, coworkers, and other folks. But sis, I suggest you reassess your approach and remember that you really don't have anything to give to others until you fill your own cup.

Life coach Paula McGee, discusses the importance of self-care in her upcoming book *Accepting Your Greatness*. Here is an excerpt from a chapter entitled "The Law of the Equal Harvest." Essentially, she suggests that you use your tragedy as an opportunity to reconnect with the Creator as well as those things that are dearest to you:

> *The truest test of our sowing comes in times of pain, suffering, tragedy, and deep disappointment. Suffering and the pain associated with it have a way of revealing the true nature and depth of our relationship with the Creator. The powerlessness, lack of control, and despair that we often feel in these situations provides an opportunity for the Creator to take a special teaching moment and birth something unique—a special harvest.*
>
> *We wonder what good could come out of these dark times. In this lonely place others are unable to meet us because of the depth of our pain. Their words of comfort do not climb over the walls of our despair. Their well-meaning condolences fall short of reaching the tender places in our heart. In these times, the Creator is calling for us to sow and trust that there are wings waiting when we choose to leave our momentary cocoon of sadness. We must be creative, even innovative, and continue to sow trust, faith, and honesty. If we do, we will find gifts that we do not expect. We will find that the Creator is birthing, creating, and developing in the midst of our heartache.*
>
> *Howard Thurman, the mystic and theologian, says that suffering calls up all of our resources. It tends to dominate our total horizon forcing us to push all else aside. The suffering becomes the great*

rallying point for energy and brings about a fight for survival either in body, in spirit, or soul. A primary demand is made upon the resources of spirit, and we come to a point of focus. He argues that the normal response to such suffering is hostility—hostility toward persons responsible for the suffering and also hostility toward the Creator.

If we are courageous enough to take our hostility to the Creator and say directly how we feel completely and thoroughly, to sow true honesty, then Thurman states that there is a "kind of ultimate suction that takes place which empties us completely." Out of this emptiness, we can find or reap insight into our suffering, quiet assurance, or we may find a way to relax our intent into the Creator's divine purpose. He suggests that suffering is the conduit that prepares us for a unique encounter with the Creator.

In these difficult times, we can also choose to sow anger, bitterness, and resentment, all of which are very easy choices when we are faced with tragedy and deep disappointment. Choosing these negative postures will only produce more of the same—different forms and new guises—anger, bitterness, and resentment will produce an equivalent harvest.

Prayer, meditation, and self-care are also available so that we can prepare for something different. We can continue to talk with the Creator and carve out quiet time to hear our own spirits. Self-care can ensure that we move forward and not be devastated by the heartache. Self-care is carving out time to sow and invest in our dreams and hopes even in the midst of the devastating pain. It may mean writing the book, finishing the portrait, or simply journaling each morning. This kind of self-care is courageous and often difficult when we find ourselves hurting.

For Debrena Jackson Gandy self-care means looking good and staying connected spiritually. When she was going through challenges in her marriage, people marveled at how great she looked. "When you're going through stuff, you don't have to look like it!" she'd respond, believing that 2003 was probably her most challenging time yet. "It's not about putting on a mask. I'm talking about self-care and nurturing your body. Taking care of yourself is crucial when you're going through tough times. And when tragedy strikes, that's when we should be the most nurtured and pampered. If we're praying and deep in meditation and introspection, then our countenance should look better than ever. But often, the very opposite happens."

For me, self-care is reaching out and supporting other people. As far as I'm concerned, I was given life so I can teach others to live. I know I was put on the planet to help people discover their precious gifts and help women feel good about their bodies. I was put here to help others see the good in every situation. I was put here to minister to anyone willing to listen to God's message. And I was put here to help my mate go from being a great husband to an awesome husband and to enable my children to recognize the greatness that lies within them. I could have chosen to die but through God's grace I've found the strength to live and help others step into a brighter tomorrow.

Like me, your mission may not be revealed overnight. I continue to be a work in progress. But have you thought about the things you would do if you knew you were faced with your final days? Would you spend more time with your family? Pursue an entrepreneurial venture? Write a book? Laugh more? Love more? Take better care of yourself? Make a list (yes, another list) and rank them by importance. Then meditate on those ideas and develop a strategy to pursue them. Take it a step further by committing to doing those activities on a regular basis—in other words stop putting off that phone call to Mom. You'll find that focusing on your own needs isn't as complicated or selfish as you once thought. In fact, the more you enjoy your life, the more joy you'll be able to give others and the hard times that you're currently experiencing may become more manageable.

OH, THE POSSIBILITIES!

Still looking for possibilities? Start doing something that you love so much that you'd actually do if for free. That's how I discovered my talent as an aerobics instructor. Initially, I taught aerobics for free at Bowie State (my alma mater). Then I taught for $4.45 an hour. Now I can make anywhere from $75 to $225 per hour teaching aerobics. But doing it for free taught me to respect and perfect my craft. Take it from me, if you concentrate on doing what you love, the payoff will follow. Also, try to use this tragedy that you're now going through for something good. When author Monique Brown got over her struggle with her fibroid, she used her experience to help others in the same predicament:

Next week, I'll actually celebrate my four-month anniversary of marriage. Since we started dating we've always made a big deal out of all anniversaries, even the little ones. As I look back on my life, it seems almost too incredible to fathom. It was only four short years ago that I was going through the most trying time of my life.

The drama started years before when I finally found out that the bleeding I was experiencing between periods was due to fibroids. I had never even heard of a fibroid. But soon those menacing growths in my uterus became a part of my everyday vocabulary. My doctor tried to convince me that fibroids are no big deal since they are not cancerous and just about every black woman you know has them, but I found that this medical condition was too big to ignore. The bleeding, which started off as a leaky-faucet sensation graduated to a longer, heavier flow, would cause my periods to run into each other. My cramps were so strong that I was nearly blinded by them. To make matters worse, the numerous doctors I saw for relief could only offer me birth control pills as a solution. One a day. Then two a day. Then as much as three to four pills a day. My varying hormone levels were causing me to feel really moody. And since these were estrogen-based birth control pills and estrogen is the agent that causes the fibroids to grow, my uterus was steadily increasing in size from the growing fibroids. The symptoms were getting worse and I watched my life become a daily misery.

As an alternate attempt to provide me with relief, a doctor performed a procedure (a myolysis) that was fairly new at that time. It was designed to cut off the blood supply from the fibroids and thus stop their accelerated growth. My doctor had only performed a few others and didn't have any feedback about the results over the long term but I was willing to take the risks, if it meant a less invasive procedure that wouldn't result in a hysterectomy. The procedure worked—temporarily. For the next two years, I was virtually fibroid-free, or so it seemed. But as with anything else, if you keep doing the same things, you keep getting the same results. I stuck with the poor exercise and dietary habits, and I stuck with a stress-filled relationship that was going nowhere. My fibroids returned, with a vengeance. The pain was three times worse than it was years earlier. There was more bleeding, resulting in severe anemia. The pain made it difficult for me to stand for long periods of time. And my uterus was the size of a five-month pregnancy. One doctor told me that I was headed for a hysterectomy, even though I was only twenty-nine years old and had no children. Now, you'd think that after five years, my boyfriend—who called himself my fiancé— would have shown his support. Not a chance. I found out through a cousin of his, that he'd fathered a child by someone else. When I confronted him with the news, in front of his prospective teenage bride, he looked at me like I had two heads, telling me that he had broken up with me years ago (which wasn't true) and that he couldn't understand why I was acting as if I didn't know about his three-month-old daughter because he'd told me about it on several occasions (which also wasn't true). I was stunned, angry, and hurt.

I fell into a deep depression. I cried. I screamed. I moped around my apartment and distanced myself from my life. As far as I was concerned, my relationship was failing me, my body was failing me, and I was failing myself. I thought of killing myself but I was afraid of going to hell. So, I muddled through each day wondering when I would ever get relief. Unlike most people, I didn't pray for God to get me through the day. I prayed that God would help me get through each step. Literally, I'd walk down the street asking God to help me make it to the stop sign, then across the street and then to the end of the block. Somehow, I'd make it to the train station, go to work and get through the day—only to start the whole process over again. Finally, a friend came to my rescue and helped me make some decisions about my health and about my life. Together we conducted some research and I decided to go ahead with a myomectomy, a surgery where the fibroids were removed and the uterus was left intact. The surgery went well and doctors were able to save my uterus. I was relieved and ready to start my new life.

During my recovery, I decided that I would write a book about my experience so that other sisters wouldn't have to go through the same horrible fibroid saga that I did. The book, It's a Sistah Thing: A Guide to Understanding and Dealing with Fibroids for Black Women *is a great success. I travel across the United States talking to sisters about fibroids and other issues. It's been one of the most exciting, yet rewarding, experiences of my life. Along the way, I've met and married the man of my dreams. Currently, we're trying to start our family and are having a sensational time enjoying each other's company. Who would have thought in the midst of all that suffering that all of these blessings were just around the corner? Now, as I tell my story to women who are going through their own trials, I let them know how important it is that they see their tragedies through to the end and never give up. If I would have given up, I would have never known that the best was yet to come.*

Sis, if this latest challenge has caused you to stomp out your dreams, I beg you to consider another point of view. There were times in my life when I didn't believe I deserved my dreams. A tragedy can make us feel unworthy and undeserving of things that are divinely ours. Trust me, a rich future is yours, just for the taking. Love yourself, pamper yourself, and start releasing the dreams stored in the lockbox of your heart.

Step 8

Pay It Forward

Shellie with her husband, Abdeltif, and her son, Amir

11/18/03

Every time I even think about doing a selfish act, I get a flashback reminding me of how important it is to give back. I first discovered this lesson when I moved to New York. I was twenty-three years old, living in Brooklyn. I wanted so much to be somebody but I had a lot of growing up to do.

My first job was at Living Well Lady as a floor person and substitute instructor, making only $4.45 an hour. I would take the D train from Brooklyn every evening up to a station at West 50th Street and Broadway, where I'd pass a homeless guy on my way to work. He'd have his hand out and I would just walk by because I was barely making it myself. But, day after day, week after week, he'd still be there.

Then, I started having problems with the people that I was staying with in Brooklyn. I was told to find another place to live but I had no place to go. To make matters worse, the person I was living with also told me I couldn't use her phone, either. I was really upset and depressed.

That day, when I passed the old homeless man, even though I only had a quarter in change because I hadn't cashed my check yet, I gave it to him and, for some reason, I felt better. I had a good night at work, despite what was going on with my living situation. For the rest of that week, I gave the homeless guy a quarter every evening.

One day my roommate was leaving and told me again not to use her phone. But as soon as she left, the phone seemed as if it was going to ring off the hook. At first, I ignored it because I thought it might have been my roommate trying to play a trick on me. But after thirty minutes, I reluctantly answered it, thinking it might be important. It was my cousin. She wanted to know if I could watch her apartment for two to three months because she was going to be touring with a singing group. I started crying. My cousin lived in a studio apartment about five blocks away. I ran all the way to her house, got the keys, and then went back to get my things while she darted off to catch her plane. That same week, I got a job at CNN. Chris Cathcartt helped me get an interview with Myron Kandel, who hired me on the spot.

The next time I returned to my aerobics job, I noticed that the homeless man was gone. At that point, I knew God was testing me. Based on the results, it appears that I passed as I witnessed firsthand that when you give, you always get back tenfold.

We're getting to the end of our journey, sis. But your healing isn't complete until you can help someone else get through a challenging time in her life. Think about your own experience and use it to inspire another individual to take an important step toward her own healing. Maybe your support will look like the assistance that you received from others, or maybe you'll just give them a copy of this book as a gift. But, seriously, you owe it to yourself and those on your support team to ensure that you soothe someone else's pain in whatever way God inspires you.

LOOKING FOR IDEAS?

Perhaps you aren't giving as much as you'd like to because you don't know how to begin. At first, I suggest you just do something that comes easiest for you. Sometimes we get discouraged when we try to do things that may be overwhelming. For example, instead of committing to adopting a child, start by babysitting for a single mother in her time of need. Or rather than volunteering to work at a senior citizen home every Saturday, try helping out over the holidays or for a special program. You'll be more likely to honor your commitment if it's a small one and you may even become inspired to do more. Kimm McNeil, someone who had been clean from a drug and alcohol addiction for the last eighteen years, tells how she pays it forward in her everyday life:

> Paying it forward can and should be an ongoing practice. I work for a mental health agency in the department of social service. If someone comes in homeless, I take $10 out of my pocket and I give it to that person. Instead of asking them to pay me back, I tell them to help the next person. I do this mainly because there have been so many times in my life that people have helped me and I could in no way pay them back for all that they've done for me. I've always had a lot of support. During my bout with drugs, my family did an enormous amount for me. I wouldn't even know how to pay them back for certain things. Perhaps the only way I can pay them back is by helping others.

When I needed to go into rehab, my family did whatever it took to make that happen despite my terrible health insurance. When I came out of the program, I moved to Westchester County to live with my sister, who supported me. My sister or my parents would often help me out financially, and it saved my life. I literally had nothing. My housing was shot. I was unemployed. I was broke. But I had good family support.

In regaining control of my life again, my first order of business was getting employment. I had good secretarial skills, so I'd always get good jobs but the trouble was keeping them because I had a drug problem. After coming out of detox and moving to West-chester, I registered at a temp agency. My second assignment was at Pepsico. They liked my work and hired me. I also started attending twelve-step meetings at Narcotics Anonymous, which was another support system. I started saving money. Six months later, I was able to purchase a car. I started going to Fordham, which I attended for about a year. Then I went to school for substance abuse counseling. I got into the field of counseling in 1989. By this time, I was a productive member of society and did the things necessary to be a responsible adult. I lived with my sister for about seven years. During that time, I started an organization called Akiele Inc. (pronounced "A key lay").

Akiele came about, or at least the initial concept was developed, after I attended a retreat with all black women that was facilitated by a white male priest. I'd been clean from drugs and alcohol for about two years and was looking forward to the experience. But something didn't sit right with me. Here you had this weekend retreat for black women that was lead by a white male Catholic priest. Although I enjoyed the retreat, I didn't like the fact that there wasn't someone like myself leading it. I thought I could do the same thing and do it better. In February 1989 I left, intend-

ing to do my own spiritual retreat by bringing in people that I knew would be able to engage women of color. I worked along with another lady to put the wheels in motion to pull our first retreat together, and the weekend was a success.

Afterwards, however, the woman I was working with really didn't want to be bothered with it anymore. Although it wasn't my intention to have another retreat I continued to do it because the sixty women that attended our first retreat wanted more of them. So, I made them happen. Around 1991, one of the things I started saying to myself was that we needed more than a weekend retreat, maybe we could do a one day conference where we would focus on specific issues like incest or domestic violence or whatever other issues people were having. During those retreats so much was coming out that I wanted to make the business broader. So we made our retreats into a nonprofit organization and later became a 501(c)3. We incorporated in 1992 but I started the retreat back in 1989, back then it was called "Sisters in Recovery." Once our purpose broadened, we changed the name to Akiele—it means wisdom in Swahili.

The mission of Akiele is to teach and empower people of color to adopt healthy life tools by hosting retreats, one-day conferences, and working with other community-based organizations to sponsor programs. We just had a one-day conference with three hundred women, and we partnered up with the Theodore D. Young Community Center. The event brought women together to empower themselves and take personal responsibility for their lives.

What motivates me? I get phone calls or letters from people who say they have had life-changing experiences as a result of something that our organization has done. I like the fact that we offer something that is unique but positive and empowering. The amount that we charge for what we do at Akiele is minimal. If people offer to pay more, we ask them to give their money to someone else.

That's paying it forward. Also, if the attendees of our program pass on the information that we give them to someone that didn't come to our event, we're still paying it forward. Women do that all of the time.

Today, I have a twelve-year-old daughter whose middle name is Akiele. I work for a mental health agency where I'm a drug and alcohol counselor. I'm the president of Akiele. I lead a very full life and am still finishing up my bachelor's degree from Empire State College, while maintaining two or three jobs. I'm trying to bring my daughter into adulthood safely and wisely and that takes a lot of my time. I'm living my life. I don't go to church but I'm very spiritual. Most importantly, I know and understand the importance of paying it forward and I incorporate paying it forward in my life every day.

Even if you're not inspired to start some life-changing organization like the sister above, there are still a host of things that you can get involved in. If you're still short on ideas, just do what I do. Here are some of the ways I've been able to pay it forward:

- I lend support. I have a friend who is a single mother raising her three kids. I volunteer to watch her kids so she can go out to enjoy herself.

- I share someone else's struggle. I have a friend of mine who is in the midst of soul-searching. To assist her in this effort, I leave word for her to attend church with me or come over so we can pray together.

- I make conversation with people I don't know when I sense they are feeling down. Once, I met a woman in a Staples store and told her I was tired. She told me that she was scared of trying to start her own business but that this was the only thing she could do because she'd lost her job. As we exited the store, I asked her if we could pray together. She agreed. I asked God to protect and bless her business. She cried and thanked me. I cried and thanked God for bringing us together because, like her, I have been afraid of starting my own business.

- I inspire children. I often go to my nephew's school to see how he is performing. Sometimes I get good reports. Other times, I get challenging ones. Just the same, I love giving my time so I can inspire him to do better. When I started going to his school on a regular basis, I noticed I was making an impression on my nephew, his friends, as well as other children.

- I volunteer my time and have enjoyed the blessings. When I was home with my son for the first eighteen months of his life, I desperately wanted to show my gratitude by being a blessing to someone else. My son and I had so much fun together that I wanted to share my joy with someone else. So, after driving by North General Hospital, I went home to call [them] to find out if I could teach aerobics to their cancer survivors. When they asked how much I'd charge, I told them I'd do it for free. That labor of love turned into a financial blessing. Four months later, when the organization was provided with a grant, they passed it on to me in exchange for more of my work. I thanked God.

- I share my experiences. Each person to whom I tell my story has helped someone else learn to live. I have now helped thousands know what it means to survive a challenge. I share because, through my challenges, I have been able to show love for all people of all colors and in all circumstances. Through my experience, they learn to live and I learn to believe that life is worth living if I can help someone else. Telling my story is important because I know I am doing something valuable with my time on earth. I can let people know that if he gave me the gift of life, then he can do the same for them.

PSALMS 100:4–5
Enter his gates with thanksgiving and his courts with praise; give thanks to him and praise his name. For the LORD is good and his love endures forever; his faithfulness continues through all generations.

PAYING IT FORWARD COMMANDMENTS

Ready to begin? Of course you are. Giving makes the world go around and it is essential for the human experience. As we've pointed out in earlier chapters, things in our lives come full circle. So the more you give, the more you get. When you give to others, you'll notice that you are the one that gets the gift—even if you don't realize it at first. But there are a few things you should know before you begin your good deeds. Here are some points to remember about giving:

- **Thou shalt not give to receive.** You can't give with expectations. Trust me, I have tried giving so that I could get and that has only resulted in frustration. What a waste of time and energy. There have been times when I missed the blessings that God put before me because I was focused on getting something else. Plus, giving to receive puts God in a box. God has the power to provide us with much more than we could ever imagine, so we cheat ourselves when we try to predict what we think we deserve.

- **Thou shalt give without regret.** When you give, don't look back and dwell on it. Your objective should be to help someone in need, and, once you've accomplished that, move on.

- **Thou shalt give thoughtfully.** You've heard the saying, what you do comes back to you. So be sure that when you do give, you do so with your whole heart and treat that person the way you'd want someone else to treat you.

- **Thou shalt allow others to service you.** Just like you shouldn't give to receive, you shouldn't receive with the intention to payback. I remember a friend who always bought me birthday, Christmas, or "just because" gifts. I felt compelled to buy her something and for years I participated in the receive-and-then-give cycle. The thing was, she had the money to give generously. I didn't. But one day, she asked me to do something expensive. I got furious with her because I knew I didn't have that kind of money, but I ended up doing it anyway. I attended the event and was miserable. Eventually, we spoke about it and she said to me, "I wasn't expecting anything from you. I gave to you because you have helped me in so many ways become strong, do some soul searching, and believe in myself." According to her, giving gifts was her only way of showing me she had something to offer. From that day forward, I decided only to give that which I have to give or can afford. I am no longer a slave to folks who give to me.

- **Thou shalt give until it helps.** Even though you shouldn't give until it puts you in financial or personal jeopardy, you should give as much as you can to help the person in need. Ensure that when you give, you do so with the intention of helping someone else not just making yourself feel good.

- **Thou shalt give with no strings attached.** One day I saw a book that I knew a friend of mine would really enjoy. I bought it, wrapped it, and hoped that it would cheer her up. She was happy when she received the book and then asked if I minded if she gave the book to someone that she knew in the hospital. I immediately said, "No, especially if it would bring your friend the same joy that it has brought you." She thanked me and put the book back in the wrapping and put her friend's name on it. So, not only did I give her joy, but that joy was passed on to someone else. Remember, you can't tell someone how to use a gift that you give them. Once you give someone a gift, they can do what they want with it.

WORDS TO STRIVE BY

Remember, I said that your acts of kindness don't have to be extravagant. I meant it. You can start caring for others by simply passing on an article that they'd be interested in or sending them a few kind words. If you're at a loss for words, I'm giving you permission to borrow from my own personal list of inspirational sayings. My Shellie-isms (provided below) are designed for you to share with the people in your life. They may be friends, family members, coworkers, or even strangers. If they look like they need inspiration, send them—via e-mail, telephone, snail mail, or pony express—some gems from my own personal power pack. These sayings won't solve their problems but they may give them the push they need to seek out solutions and expect results.

- I belong in the front.

- My lips, butt, hands, and feet are big and beautiful.

- Give when you love; give when you hurt.

- When the world says "no," you say "yes!"

Paying forward can be as simple as zapping someone an e-mail. Although I don't know who wrote this, when I received it, I found it to be a great mood booster. I hope it does the same for you and the people on your e-mail list.

Living

There are moments in life when you miss someone so much that you just want to pick them from your dreams and hug them for real! When the door of happiness closes, another opens; but oftentimes we look so long at the closed door that we don't see the one that has been opened for us.

Don't go for looks; they can deceive. Don't go for wealth; even that fades away. Go for someone who makes you smile, because it takes only a smile to make a dark day seem bright. Find the one that makes your heart smile.

Dream what you want to dream; go where you want to go; be what you want to be, because you have only one life and one chance to do all the things you want to do.

May you have enough happiness to make you sweet, enough trials to make you strong, enough sorrow to keep you human, enough hope to make you happy. The happiest of people don't necessarily have the best of everything; they just make the most of everything that comes along their way.

The brightest future will always be based on a forgotten past; you can't go forward in life until you let go of your past failures and heartaches.

When you were born, you were crying and everyone around you was smiling. Live your life so that, at the end, you're the one who is smiling and everyone around you is crying.

- I am as graceful as Susan Taylor and as rich as Oprah.

- Love everybody and you will receive love in return.

- Instead of controlling others, put God in control of your life.

- Anger grows under your skin and kills off all the good cells that are created in you.

- Since my feet are a size twelve; that means I can step into the world with a whole foot.

- It's not in me to give up.

- Sometimes losing makes you a winner.

- Freedom is being happy no matter the outcome.

- Dream on with your bad self.

- Dancing keeps me on my toes.

- Through my pain, suffering, and loss, I can serve as someone else's angel.

- I will use my pain for good.

A Word from Mom

Now I know what you're thinking. I'm Shellie's mother, so of course I'm going to use this opportunity to boast and brag about my daughter. And you are absolutely right. But I'm also going to use this space to tell the truth. I know Shellie better than anyone else. And the truth is that Shellie is a changed woman who has matured beyond her years. Believe me when I tell you, Shellie is not the person I knew less than ten years ago.

I went to see my daughter in New York before she was diagnosed with cancer. At the time, she was married and pregnant. I told her that her husband was not the one for her. I guess you could call it mother's intuition. I could tell she went through a lot of stress in that marriage, and I told her that she couldn't continue to live like that. If I had my way, I would have taken her right back home with me but there are some things that you have to let your children go through. The next time I visited her, Shellie really looked like she was on her way out. She'd just lost the baby and she took it really hard. She saw the baby and couldn't get the picture out of her mind. When we got out of the hospital and came home, she was done in. I knew it was a lot for her to bear so I asked God to tell me what to say to my daughter to help her through this. The only thing I could think of was to tell her that we should go to church where we could hear God's word. We found a church in the local newspaper. They didn't know us and we didn't know them. The next thing you know, the preacher said that God has told me to preach on forgiveness and it was directed right at my child. She had to forgive herself. She blamed herself for losing her child, and that's why she was taking it so hard. She wasn't resting and she just wasn't getting it together. We both cried because we knew God was telling Shellie to forgive herself and that the loss was not her fault. I stayed with her for a while before returning back to my home in Baltimore. Less than a year later, she told me the doctor had diagnosed her with breast cancer.

When she was diagnosed with cancer, that was a blow. She could have given up. She could have said she couldn't fight this thing. Shellie had chemo for a year—it wasn't like it was six months. They felt because she was so young that she should have the total strength of what chemo could do. If that didn't work, they were going to consider a bone marrow transplant. The experience my daughter had with cancer was terrible for me. To think that I could lose my child was more than my heart could take. I don't think I could live with losing my child. In fact, I knew I couldn't bear losing my child and I told God that. That was the truth, I couldn't. I was traveling from Baltimore to New York to be with her every weekend, but I still felt helpless. I realized how she must have felt but I couldn't do anything. I wasn't into prayer as much as she is today. And when I saw her without her hair, the hair that had grown so beautiful, I think it almost broke me. She lost all of her hair, didn't have a strand of hair from the chemo. I didn't let her see how I felt but my heart went out to my precious girl. I didn't know how she would get through it. But I felt in my heart that God wouldn't have brought us this far for him to take her from me. I was right.

God saw her through it, gave her support, and connected her to good friends. He helped her deal with the hard times that came with treatment, like losing her hair and seeing her own friends die from cancer. He blessed her with Ms. Marie, a woman who became like a real mother to her. I thank God for her: She was a big help, since Shellie was living in a city where she didn't have any real family. Ms. Marie was a strong woman and when she saw my daughter giving way to cancer, she wouldn't let her do it. I could always call Ms. Marie and ask how is my baby doing. And she'd keep me posted.

Then Shellie started changing. She wasn't afraid anymore. She told me she was getting support from her friends and she started exercising and doing things. She told me that God had been talking to her. Those things had never happened to me. During that time, Shellie became very close to God. She even taught me things that helped me. It seemed she was being transformed. She stopped biting her tongue and didn't procrastinate anymore. And all of the things she'd lost, were gradually being reintroduced to her life. As you know, she now has a wonderful husband, a little boy, a great job, a stable life, and another bundle on the way. These are all of the things I wanted her to have. These are the things I'd prayed for. And this experience that she's had with cancer has turned into a positive thing. I don't think she could have learned what she has or be where she is right now without it. Instead of being bitter, Shellie's turned the whole experience into something great. She has touched the lives of many women, and I feel privileged to witness and learn from her journey.

My daughter didn't use my mistakes in life as an excuse to fail herself. She could have, because children tend to emulate what their parents do. My marriage to her father didn't work. When I got married, I didn't know how to be a wife so I couldn't show my daughter how to be one. My ex-husband and I loved each other very much. But we didn't know how to care for each other, and we never learned. If I had to do it over again, I would have tried to seek some type of counseling for my husband and myself. But God knows best. After the divorce, I was lonely and I was in a relationship that was wrong for me. The man didn't treat me like he should have and I shouldn't have even been in it. I asked God to give me the strength to stop selling myself short. But it took time.

It was a cycle. Sometimes when you have setbacks, your children have setbacks. My mother and father broke up when I was only three years old. I was raised by my father's people. He left me with my grandmother, and she didn't have time to nurture me because she'd already nurtured thirteen children. When you come from a broken home, there are so many things that come with that. I took those experiences with me into adulthood.

When Shellie got cancer, the cycle was broken. God allowed those things to happen to my daughter so that he could give her the wisdom that she needs early rather than later in life. What she has already accomplished could have taken her twenty years instead of ten. God didn't want my daughter to have the setbacks in life that I had, so he allowed cancer to happen to her so that she might have a good life and help others.

Shellie isn't just saying things that sound good. When she tells you to P.U.S.H. (pray until something happens), she really lives that. Prayer is something that my daughter has talked to me about. I guess having to face the fact that she might die scared her. Shellie wasn't into prayer before she got sick. She was a different person than what she is today.

She's also being authentic when she tells you to "get an attitude of gratitude." I remember going to her house one day and I saw all of these thank-you cards. I asked her about them. She told me that a young lady she met was really nice to her, so she got her address and was planning to send her a thank-you card. She wanted the woman to know that she appreciated just knowing her. And that's the way she is now. When people do things for her, or even if she just sees someone and shakes their hand, she sends them a card. When she does that, they respond. Maybe a month later, they would send her a letter back and say thank you. Now Shellie appreciates the little things even more than a brand-new coat. At one time, it wasn't like that. It seems like it's the little things that she wants now. It really is something. She's very appreciative and this cancer has really changed her.

Her whole life is about "paying forward." Once a friend of mine asked my daughter to talk to someone else who had cancer because this woman blamed cancer for every negative thing that was happening in her life. Shellie spoke to the woman but there was so much bitterness in that young woman, and even though she knew that she was facing death, she stayed in the house all of the time, with closed doors and windows. The lady wasn't willing to receive and she died last year. That struck my daughter and furthered her commitment to let people know what cancer really is. All of the experiences that she's had from her broken marriage to her experience with chemo, and everything in between, brought her to where she is right now. I believe that God has a special thing for my daughter to do and this is all part of it.

She's not perfect, she makes mistakes but she truly wants to help somebody and she wants the women out there to know that they can make it and succeed. Despite her shortcomings, Shellie is still helping other people strive for a better life as she continues on her path of development. Prayer has really helped Shellie deal with her personal challenges, and my daughter says, through prayer, I can conquer some of my shortcomings as well. I'm working on them, have prayed about them, and some of my shortcomings have gone away. But there are some people that have shortcomings who don't want people to tell them about it. Sometimes we only admit the shortcomings to ourselves.

But when you are confronted with those shortcomings you need to do something about them. That's how Shellie deals with them: She overcomes her faults.

Shellie is also committed to improving herself in various areas. Now she has become a fabulous cook. That was not something that she was good at. Homegirl is also trying to sing. She's doing things that I never thought she could do. She proves that if you can dream it, you can achieve it.

So don't think Shellie is only an inspiration for you; she has been a good support system for me, too. I'm fifty-seven years old and she is telling *me* some things now. It's because of her that I now believe I can do something serious with my life. I'm grateful. She's become more than just a daughter and I thank God for her.

Tragic things happen sometimes in order to bring God's people where He wants them to be. Sometimes it seems like a roundabout way. But God has blessed my daughter because, at a young age, she has acquired wisdom well beyond her years. In the Bible, Solomon chose wisdom over wealth, and because he did that, God blessed him with both. I think that's the plan for Shellie, too.

A lot of sisters need to hear her. I know I do. Our women are in trouble. They are seeking happiness in the wrong churches, in the arms of the wrong men, and in the wrong things. Shellie is a mature woman, believes in God, and is a shining example for all of us.

Finally, I think it's great that she is leaving a legacy behind. I've had people in my family that have attempted to write books or stories but they haven't come about yet. I had an aunt whom my daughter was crazy about. But when that aunt passed away, she had twenty pages of something she tried to write but never finished. I know that Shellie won't leave her tasks incomplete because she's on a mission. I'm just grateful that we can all see her story unfold.

Okay, so I did use this space as a place to further celebrate the accomplishments of my daughter. But can you blame me?

Afterword

I guess you're wondering how everything has turned out. So much is going on, I don't even know where to begin. Prior to cancer, I wanted to have a husband with two kids, travel around the world, be a television talk show host, and change the world. Even after my illness, I never let go of my dreams.

At thirty-seven years old, I'm seeing them come to pass. You already know that I've married the man of my dreams and have a wonderful son, but the rabbit has died again. Sis, I took the pregnancy test so early that I could barely see the pink line but it was there. I was pregnant—indeed! What a blessing. Abdeltif and I have been trying to conceive another baby for three months. After we lost our last baby, we figured this was the one prayer that wouldn't get answered. Ah, but our dream of being "parents-squared" has begun to manifest.

Public speaking is still a priority for me. I continue to tell women,

men, and children about living life to the fullest. When people hear the saying "to whom much is given, much is required," they really don't realize what that means. But I'm going to spend the rest of my days helping people define that saying for themselves. I beat a death sentence, and I'm going to spend my life being grateful for my second chance. I could have chosen to die but I chose to teach an aerobics class and inspire people to improve their way of living in the process. My speaking engagements have taken me across the country, and I look forward to doing more of them in the future. And since this blessing is growing by leaps and bounds, I know I'm assured to take this message to other countries, too. I'm just relying on God to help me make the right connections.

I am happier than I ever dreamed possible. I guess that's primarily because I finally believe I deserve it. Sometimes we choose to be unhappy without even realizing it. I'm no longer claiming a life of despair. I'm too powerful for that. I know now that happiness is a personal choice.

It's unfortunate that I had to endure a series of trials—being raised by a single parent, divorce, illness, and losing two children—before I learned some very important life lessons. But I was angry, resentful, frustrated, and fearful. I allowed all of those things to hinder me from achieving true success. I pursued people, places, and things that ultimately blocked my true potential. I think God had to do something really drastic if he was ever going to get my attention. Fortunately, I overcame those challenges. But I did it so that you wouldn't have to suffer the same consequences. Learn from my mistakes. Love yourself, love God, and love the people that cross your path.

And if you are in the midst of a struggle, be encouraged. No matter how serious the situation, I'm proof that you can come out on top. God's wish for you is far greater than you can even imagine. Just hold on to his unchanging hand, follow the steps in this book, and keep the faith. Know that you will survive this heartbreak as long as you never give up on yourself or your dreams.

Good Luck and God Bless,
Shellie

Appendix A

Information About Sisters and Breast Cancer—Some Facts You Should Know

- Breast cancer is the most common cancer among black women, with an estimated 20,000 new cases in 2003.

- Cancerous tumors are more likely to be larger in black women.

- It's estimated that approximately 5,700 African-American women died from breast cancer in 2003.

- Overall, black women are less likely to be diagnosed with breast cancer than white (non-Hispanic) women but they have a higher death rate than white women. Among African-American women, 73 percent of them live past the five-year survival rate as compared to 88 percent of white women. In addition, younger African-American women (under age 40) have a higher incidence of breast cancer than their white counterparts (although the incidence of getting breast cancer under age 40 is low among all ethnicities).

- The survival gap between white and black women is widening. The death rate for African-American women is 30 percent higher than that of their white counterparts.

WHY SISTERS AREN'T GETTING TREATED SOON ENOUGH (AND WHY THOSE EXCUSES DON'T HOLD UP)

1. You fear losing your breast. The earlier you seek treatment, the less likely you'll have to get a mastectomy—breast removal. If the cancer has not spread and the tumor is small, then the growth as well as the tissue surrounding it may be removed by a lumpectomy, a method that leaves the breast intact. To destroy the remaining cancer cells, radiation therapy and chemotherapy may be used.

2. You are basing your decision on misinformation. Contrary to popular belief:

- Mammograms do not cause cancer.

- Women with small breasts or large breasts are both at risk.

- You cannot get breast cancer from a blow (hit).

- Surgery does not cause cancer cells to spread.

- High caffeine consumption has not been proven to cause cancer.

- Keloids do not increase cancer risk.

3. You are afraid that cancer treatments will cause you to lose your job. Since many African-American women are typically the head of the household, they worry about loss of income if they miss work as a result of being treated for cancer. However, early diagnosis and treatment can help to ensure that the patient returns to her normal activities in a relatively short time.

4. You are not aware of the risks. Cancer is not a white women's disease; black women get breast cancer, too. Also, you don't have to have a family history of breast cancer to get it. Approximately 80 percent of women who are diagnosed don't have breast cancer in their family.

Proven Risk Factors

- Female

- Over the age of 50

- Family history, especially mother, sister, daughter, or other first-degree relative

- No children (nulliparity)

- First full-term pregnancy after age 30

- Early menarche (first period) before age 12

- Late menopause (after age 50)

- Genetic test findings associated with breast cancer

- Exposure to high-dose ionizing radiation (for cancer, acne, thyroid)

Potential Risk Factors

- Tall stature and heavy frame

- Obesity after menopause

- Alcohol intake over nine drinks per week

- History of high alcohol intake before age 30

- Exposure to prolonged use of high-dose estrogen

- Diet: low fiber, low antioxidants, low zinc, low selenium

- Lack of exercise, especially before age 40

- Environmental hazard exposure

5. You're not sure how cancer develops. Cancer develops when the cells start to divide uncontrollably and form masses called tumors. Since breast cancer grows slowly, the disease may have occupied your body for some time before you actually feel a mass. Yearly mammogram (an X-ray of the breast) can detect tiny growths in their early stages before you're able to feel them in your breast. The earlier cancer is detected, the more likely the patient can be cured.

6. You don't have health insurance coverage. No problem, there are many organizations offering free or low-cost mammograms. For referrals, contact the American Cancer Society, 1-800-ACS-2345, www.cancer.org, or the National Cancer Institute, 1-800-4-CANCER.

7. You think you're too young to have a mammogram. Since breast cancer occurs at a younger age in African-American women, the American Cancer Society suggests that black women start getting regular mammograms at age 30 or at age 25, if there is a family history of the disease. Beyond that, women should perform breast self-exams on a regular basis and look for these symptoms:

- A mass in the breast (even though many lumps are benign or noncancerous, they should still be evaluated by a physician)

- Discharge from the nipple

- An inverted nipple
- Dimpling of the skin on the breast

BREAST CANCER IS NOT A WHITE WOMEN'S DISEASE: A Q&A WITH DR. HAROLD FREEMAN

(Dr. Harold Freeman is the medical director of the Ralph Lauren Center for Cancer Care and Prevention. To contact the Ralph Lauren Cancer Center for patient advocacy and other services, call 212-987-1777.)

Why do black women have a lower incidence of breast cancer when compared to white women?

There are theories, but we don't really know the cause of breast cancer. The most likely cause of the difference may be related to childbearing. The time that women give birth to children would be one factor. Black women, in general, tend to have children at a younger age than white women in this country. When women have children at an early age it is somewhat of a protective factor against breast cancer. In populations of women who tend to have children at a younger age, there is a lower incidence of breast cancer. This may be one explanation as to why black women have a lower incidence overall than white women.

Why do black women with breast cancer tend to have a shorter life span than their white counterparts?

Yes, black women do have a greater chance of dying from the disease. We say they have a higher mortality. Black women have a higher mortality (death rate) because they are diagnosed at later stages of the disease. They come in late for treatment, often at a point where not as many of them are cured.

Why do black women come in later for treatment?

That is mainly related to the poverty rate between black and white women. Black people tend to have lower economic status than white people. The poverty rate from the U.S. Census Bureau reported that 24 percent of black Americans are poor, meaning that, in a family of four, their income is below $18,000 a year. Where only 8 percent of white people live below the poverty line.

Another issue is lack of insurance. Among African Americans, 21 percent are uninsured compared to 10 percent of white Americans. So factors related to economics play a big role in determining who gets into the system early for early diagnosis and treatment. Black people are poorer and tend to be less insured than white people. I believe that is the most important reason why blacks come in later and are treated later.

Is there any way we can reduce the risks of breast cancer?

We don't know how to reduce the risk of breast cancer as far as I know. We do know how to diagnose it early and treat it properly. With this information, we can reduce the death rate in black women if they come in early for treatment.

Can breast cancer be cured?

In breast cancer, the standard that we use to indicate that someone is cured is probably at least ten years from the time of treatment with no evidence of recurrent disease. There may be a small percentage of women who would have recurrence after that. If someone has no recurrence after ten years from the time of primary treatment, that's when we consider them to be cured, with a few exceptions. I've seen many people cured. We have twenty- or thirty-year cures.

Can people who have been treated for breast cancer still have children?

I think that having kids after radiation is not rare. Radiation is directed to the breast area. As far as chemotherapy is concerned, it depends on how much chemo and what dosages are given to the patient. A woman could lose ovarian function permanently, but it depends on the dosages. Still, I've seen women who have had children [even after chemo]. But most women who develop breast cancer are 40 and above and not many women have children after they are 40. I have, however, seen women who have developed breast cancer at an early age and they have children after treatment.

Do you recommend women have children after breast cancer?

You have to weigh the whole picture. Every case is individual and it would depend on the woman being fully informed about the possible risks of having children. A baby drives your estrogen way up during pregnancy. Most studies don't show that having children after breast cancer is dangerous. The current opinion in science is that if you have no evidence of recurrent disease after several years, then the patient could have children. It's been a debated point among sciences. But it depends on how much that woman values having children.

What are the newest developments for the treatment of breast cancer?

The latest development is that women can be treated for breast cancer with breast preservation. Now we have studies that prove in clinical trials that a lumpectomy (removing the lump and leaving the breast intact) is equal to the removal of the total breast for women who have breast cancers that are small.

How does having a positive attitude impact one's chances for recovery?

I don't think we know enough about that. I don't know of any evidence that attitude can affect your healing. It's a difficult thing to study. But attitude can probably affect your quality of life. Your quality of life can be influenced by your attitude.

What can women do (outside of getting medical treatment) to increase their chances of recovering from breast cancer?

The main thing that can impact your recovery is the stage the disease is at when you get diagnosed and treated. Get diagnosed early so your treatment is not as radical. Not everybody gets the proper treatment for breast cancer, but the quality of the treatment is very important to determining how well you do.

What resources do you recommend for people overcoming breast cancer?

Support is very helpful. A woman who has a mammogram that's abnormal needs to have a support system to make sure she gets a biopsy and the proper treatment. Support systems can help her navigate this very complicated health system. Patient navigation is very important. From the point where she has a suspicious finding through treatment, women need to get support to help them navigate through the system to overcome barriers that prevent the proper treatment.

So, what's the bottom line here?

The issue is that, although black women have a slightly lower incidence of breast cancer, they also have a higher death rate; and the higher death rate is related to socioeconomic status, including poverty, leading to lack of education, which leads to lack of access to health care for an early diagnosis. There is nothing innate about being black that causes you to have a higher death rate from cancer. You may save your life by seeking early treatment.

BREAST CANCER SELF-EXAMINATION

Early detection is key as far as breast cancer is concerned. One highly effective way of detecting the early signs of breast cancer is by regular gynecologic checkups and monthly self-exams. Here is how you can check your breasts for important changes:

In the Shower

Raise one arm. With fingers flat, touch every part of each breast, gently feeling for a lump or thickening. Use your right hand to examine your left breast, your left hand for your right breast.

Before a Mirror

With arms first at your sides, then raised above your head, look carefully for changes in the size, shape, and contour of each breast. Look for puckering, dimpling, or changes in skin texture. Gently squeeze both nipples and look for discharge.

Lying Down

Place a towel or pillow under your right shoulder and put your right hand behind your head. Examine your right breast with your left hand.

Fingers flat, press gently in small circles, starting at the outermost top edge of your breast and spiraling in toward the nipple. Examine every part of the breast. Repeat with left breast.

Standing Up

With your arm resting on a firm surface, use the same circular motion to examine the underarm area. This is breast tissue, too.

If you notice any indications of possible breast cancer, see your doctor. Clinical procedures to detect breast cancer may include a breast cancer exam and mammography.

BENIGN BREAST CANCER PROBLEMS

There are various problems that can occur with your breasts that aren't cancerous. The most common issues of non-cancerous breast problems are lumps and thickening, breast pain, nipple discharge, and breast infections.

Lumps and Thickenings

The signs: If you come across a breast lump or thickening, you might wait a week or through one menstrual cycle and then recheck your breast. If you still feel it, call your doctor or nurse practitioner.

Treatment: Your doctor or nurse practitioner will initially examine both breasts. Then they'll indicate if you need further testing. If you do need more testing, you'll probably have diagnostic tests like a mammography, ultrasonography, cytology (needle aspiration studies), or biopsy (histology). If a biopsy is performed, it could come in the form of office core or fine-needle aspiration biopsy, stereotactic biopsy (Mammotone or ABBI, a less invasive procedure), ultrasound-guided biopsy, or excisional biopsy in the operating room under local anesthesia or sedation.

Nipple Discharge

The signs: Typically, nipple discharges are associated with aging (ductal ectasia) or hormonal changes. During your self-examination or other manipulation, you may get nipple discharge that may infrequently occur in the form of tiny drops. This form of discharge is common. A less common condition, however, is persistent nipple discharge that is spontaneous and/or is released in measurable amounts. If you're experiencing nipple discharge, note the characteristics of it: color, consistency, amount, what activity preceded the discharge, and where the discharge comes from. All nipple discharge findings should be evaluated by a doctor.

Treatment: If a doctor does not find any abnormalities during your breast exam and appropriate screenings, then you should return for a follow-up in three to six months. If your doctor finds nipple discharge on examination, your physician will first try to determine where the discharge is coming from, see if there is blood in the fluid, and consider collecting cytology and/or bacteriology smears of the fluid. He may also want to perform a diagnostic study like a ductogram, but only when the source and location of the nipple discharge is known. One way to resolve discharge is through wedge resection of the involved sub-areolar area of the breast. But persistent or recurrent nipple discharge could indicate a papillary cancer. However, most nipple discharge is not cancerous.

Breast Pain

The signs: Breast pain could occur at almost any age and could be associated with a variety of conditions. If you have breast pain, classify it by determining if the pain is one-sided or bilateral, constant or intermittent, frequent or occasional, sharp, dull, aching, knife-like, or "sticking" sensations. All of these descriptions are typical. Typically, breast pain is due to either hormonal changes associated with menstruation, pregnancy, perimenopause, and/or menopause or muscular strains of the chest wall, upper back, and shoulder muscles.

Treatment: Your doctor will thoroughly examine the breasts, lymph nodes, and muscles of the chest and shoulders to determine whether you need such diagnostic tests as mammography, sonography, or needle aspiration of cysts. Treatment may include: changing asthma medications; reducing or stopping caffeine and nicotine intake; taking different birth control or hormone pills or changing the dosage of them; or trying low-dose diuretics. There are also women who get results from certain vitamins or natural remedies which may include vitamin E (600–800 IU daily), vitamin B complex (50–100 milligrams daily) or evening primrose oil (1000–1200 milligrams daily). The use of tincture of thyme may provide some relief to perimenopausal women who experience rapid hormonal changes. For mild pain, or before your doctor's visit, you may want to try medications such as Ibuprofen or Acetaminophen. Also wear a good support bra and try heat or cold packs (use whatever works for you). In very severe cases of breast pain, your doctor may recommend strong hormones (e.g., Lupron or Danazol), which temporarily prevents the ovary function, for relief.

Breast Infections

The signs: This condition is relatively uncommon. When it does occur, the pain is either generalized, where the woman's whole breast hurts or throbs, or is localized, where the breast hurts in a particular area. Generalized breast pain (mastitis) is typically associated with breast-feeding, pregnancy, or radiation of the breast during cancer treatment. While localized breast infection is frequently associated with abscess, cellulitis (a noncontagious infection of the connective tissue beneath the skin), folliculitis (contagious inflammation or infection of one or more hair follicles of the skin), or other skin or soft tissue lesions. Just like other infections, infections in the breast can become very serious where they cause high fevers or can trigger other illness. It's extremely important that breast infections be treated immediately.

Treatment: Breast infections are typically treated with antibiotics. Other treatments could include heat, pain relievers, and surgical incision, and drainage. If surgery occurs, your doctor or nurse practitioner should advise you on caring for the wound, and a series of follow-up visits may be required.

Appendix B

Resources for Women with Breast Cancer

- Get connected to free services and support by contacting SHARE: 212-719-0364 and the Sisters Network: 516-538-8086.

- For free mammograms and other cancer screenings, contact Black Examination Center of Harlem: 212-531-8000.

- Breast cancer facts and figures, 2003–2004, are available by calling toll free 1-800-ACS-2345 (1-800-227-2345) and or logging onto www.cancer.org.

ON THE WEB

African American Women's Resource Center	www.AAWRC.org
Black Women for Wellness	www.BWWLA.com
Black Women's Network	www.Blackliving.com
Black Women's Health	www.BlackWomensHealth.com
Ask Dr. Ro	www.DrRoGear.com and www.askdrro.com

Janice Ferebee	www.JaniceFerebee.com
Mocha Moms	www.MochaMoms.org
NIA ONLINE	www.NIAONLINE.com
National Cancer Institute	www.nci.nih.gov
Black Women's Health Imperative	www.NBWHP.com
Onyx Woman Magazine	www.OnyxWoman.com
Positive Women Uniting	www.PWUniting.com
TC's Sista Circle	www.SistaCircle.com
Daily Affirmations for Sistas	www.SistaPower.com
Connecting Urban Professionals	www.Urban-Union.com
Women Who Dare: Cards, Gifts and Bookstore	www.GreetingsFrom WomenWhoDare.com
Woman2Woman Social Group	www.W2W2000.com
Low-cost Web and graphic design	www.eytihia.com

ORGANIZATIONS FOR BREAST CANCER SURVIVORS

African American Women in Touch
(574) 284-6944
http://www.qualityoflife.org
This organization encourages African Americans to more actively participate in their healthcare needs.

American Breast Cancer Foundation
(877) 539-2543
http://www.abcf.org
This organization sponsors the American Breast Cancer Foundation's Key to Life Breast Cancer Screening Assistance Program, which provides free breast cancer screenings to women who cannot afford them. Also, women who qualify can participate in their local Center for Disease Control breast- and cervical-cancer-screening programs.

ABC/African-American Breast Cancer Group of the Central Coast
www.armelitas@sbcglobal.net

African-American Breast Cancer Alliance, Inc.
www.geocities.com/aabcainc
(612) 825-3675.

Association of Black Psychologists
(for leads)
www.abpsi.org
(202) 722-0808

Breast Cancer Action
(415) 243-9301
(800) 387-9816
http://www.bcaction.org
This organization aims to end the breast cancer epidemic by influencing changing public policies.

Breast Cancer Action Nova Scotia
(902) 465-2685
http://www.bcans.com/index.htm
BCANS, a nonprofit breast cancer advocacy/support group, provides services for breast cancer survivors. It is funded by the Breast Cancer Fund and the Canadian Breast Cancer Foundation.

Breast Cancer Resource Committee
(202) 463-8040
http://www.afamerica.com/bcrc
Informs and educates the African-American community about breast cancer by advocating for organizations that promote the importance of early detection and treatment.

Breastcancer.org
http://www.breastcancer.org
This Web site provides life-saving information so women can understand what breast cancer is, how it develops, and ways it may be prevented.

Canadian Breast Cancer Foundation
(416) 596-6773
(800) 387-9816
http://www.cbcf.org
Focuses on research, diagnosis, and treatment for breast cancer.

Community Breast Health Project
(650) 326-6686 Helpline
http://www.med.stanford.edu/CBHP
Operates as a clearinghouse for information, support, and resources for any-one touched by breast cancer. Find out about volunteer opportunities and lo-cal support groups that are located in Palo Alto, California.

Florida Breast Cancer Coalition
(305) 669-0011
(877) 644-FBCC
http://www.fbccoalition.org
Grassroots organization that tries to obtain government funding for breast cancer research. Member of NBCC.

Georgia Breast Cancer Coalition
(770) 452-7988
http://www.gabcc.org
Provides Georgians with an organizational platform from which to educate the public and increase research funds to eradicate breast cancer. Member of NBCC.

Huntington Breast Cancer Action Coalition
(613) 547-1518
http://www.hbcac.org
The organization promotes breast cancer awareness, advocacy, education, and support. Member of NBCC.

Hurricane Voices
(617) 928-3300
(866) 667-3300

http://www.hurricanevoices.org
Hurricane Voices raises awareness, promotes activities, and supports events to find the cause of and cure for breast cancer.

Linda Creed Breast Cancer Foundation
(215) 545-0800
http://www.lindacreed.org
Committed to empowering women and their families to practice breast health, learn about detection, and understand treatment options. The foundation also strives to establish a public agenda for prevention and cure.

Massachusetts Breast Cancer Coalition
(617) 376-6222
http://www.mbcc.org
Uses activism, advocacy, and education to tackle the breast cancer epidemic.

National Alliance of Breast Cancer Organizations
(888) 80-NABCO
http://www.nabco.org
Supports a network that provides information, assistance, and referrals for questions about breast cancer. Serves as an advocate for the interests and concerns of breast cancer survivors and women at risk.

The Breast Center at Mercy
http://breastcenter.mdmercy.com
Hosts a wealth of support programs for breast cancer survivors and their families, including arm-in-arm breast cancer support meetings, Reach-to-recovery, one-on-one support group, and helping hands for cancer patients with limited financial resources. Breast care and other health information available twenty-four hours a day by calling 1-800-MD-MERCY. During normal business hours, Monday through Friday, 9 A.M. to 5 P.M., you may call the Hoffberger Breast Center at Mercy directly at 410-332-9330.

National Breast Cancer Coalition
(202) 296-7477
(800) 622-2838

http://www.natlbcc.org
Uses action and advocacy to eradicate breast cancer.

National Lymphedema Network
(510) 208-3200
(800) 541-3259
http://www.lymphnet.org
Supports lymphedema patients, health professionals, and the general public by disseminating information on the prevention and management of the illness through education and guidance.

One-In-Nine, The Long Island Breast Cancer Coalition
(516) 357-9622
http://www.1in9.org
Uses advocacy, education, outreach, and support to promote breast cancer awareness.

Race for the Cure
(800) 462-9273
http://www.raceforthecure.com
Tackles the breast cancer epidemic by education, research, advocacy, education, screening, and treatment.

Rhode Island Breast Cancer Coalition
(401) 822-7984
This advocacy organization seeks to change the world of breast cancer by working with the scientific community. Member of NBCC.

SHARE: Self-Help for Women with Breast or Ovarian Cancer
(212) 719-0364
http://www.sharecancersupport.org
Breast: 212-382-2111
Ovarian: 212-719-1204
(212) 719-4454, (Spanish)
Disseminates information on breast and ovarian cancer and helps sufferers gain more control over their lives during and after diagnosis.

Sisters In Survival SIS
http://www.sistersinsurvival.org
1(800) 925-8771

Sister's Network
(866) 781-1808
http://www.sistersnetworkinc.org
Spotlights the impact that breast cancer has on the African-American community. Its primary goals are to provide emotional and psychological support as well as resources for medical research and cancer prevention programs. You can find an affiliate in your area.

Spirit of Hope
(212) 369-3205
dgwilsondavis@aol.com

Susan G. Komen Foundation
800-IM-AWARE toll free breast hotline
http://www.komen.org
The Komen Foundation, considered the world leader in the fight against breast cancer, supports innovative research and community-based outreach programs. It works through a network of national and international affiliates and hosts events such as the Komen Race for the Cure®. It also fights to eradicate breast cancer by funding research grants, supporting education, and screening and treatment programs in communities throughout the globe.

Texas Cancer Center
(713) 975-6270
http://www.texascancercenter.com; http://cancerebook.com
The Texas Cancer Center (TCC) seeks to educate patients about the success of conservative surgery for breast cancer. The TCC also brings the medical research and clinical experience of leading cancer centers to your kitchen table in terms you can understand in the book *Cancer Breakthrough You've Never Heard Of.*

The Breast Cancer Fund
(415) 346-8226
http://www.breastcancerfund.org
Attempts to ensure that all breast cancer survivors receive the best medical care, support services, and information.

The Catherine Peachy Fund, Inc.
(219) 269-2198
Pushes for advancements in breast cancer awareness, treatment, and care by funding scientific research.

University of Wisconsin Comprehensive Cancer Center
(608) 263-8600
http://www.cancer.wisc.edu/
This center serves Wisconsin as well as adjoining areas of Iowa and Illinois; it emphasizes cancer prevention and treatments using various modalities. Also encourages patient participation in clinical trials.

Walnut Avenue Women's Center
(831) 426-3062
http://members.cruzio.com/~wawc/
The organization hosts a number of programs supporting women's issues that include topics such as teenage motherhood, family support services, food banks, domestic violence intervention, recovery strategies, and breast cancer survivors.

Women's Information Network Against Breast Cancer
(626) 332-2255
866-2WINABC (toll free)
http://www.winabc.org
Provides breast cancer patients with treatment information as well as peer support from the diagnosis to recovery.

Women of Color Breast Cancer Survivors Support Project
www.wocbcssp.net
(310) 330-5140

Women of Color (WOC) sponsors "Each One Teach One" breast health seminars that have supported more than 400 breast cancer survivors and educated at least 4,500 African-American women. The organization takes its efforts to underserved communities, where women are encouraged to examine their breasts, have mammograms, and get medical examinations. Group-support meetings are held on the second Saturday of each month from 1 P.M. to 4 P.M. at the Daniel Freeman Hospital in Inglewood, California.

Women of Essence
www.womenofessence.org
(310) 537-8227
The organization provides a strong support base and an emotional safe haven for breast cancer survivors to air their frustrations, concerns, and fears. It also educates survivors by offering updated breast cancer information so they can be more proactive in managing their health.

Y-ME: National Breast Cancer Organization
(619) 569-9283
(800) 221-2141, 800-986-9505 (Spanish)
http://www.y-me.org
Supports and informs breast cancer patients as well as their families.

Young Survival Coalition
(212) 206-6610
http://www.youngsurvival.org
This organization is the only international, nonprofit network of breast cancer survivors and supporters dealing with the concerns and issues that affect young women with breast cancer (under age 40). YSC educates the research, legislative, medical, and breast cancer communities through advocacy, action, and awareness.

BOOKS

On Breast Cancer

Breast Cancer: Black Women
by Edward T. Johnson, M.D.

Dr. Susan Love's Breast Book
by Susan M. Love, Karen Lindsey, Marcia Williams, Susan M., Md. Love

Rosen's Breast Pathology
by Paul Peter Rosen

Breast Cancer? Let Me Check My Schedule!
by Erma Bombeck

After Breast Cancer: A Common-Sense Guide to Life After Treatment
by Hester Hill Schnipper, LICSW, BCD

The Breast Reconstruction Guidebook: Issues and Answers from Research to Recovery
by Kathy Steligo

On Health

It's a Sistah Thing: A Guide to Understanding and Dealing with Fibroids For Black Women
by Monique R. Brown

My Favorite Books

Life Application Bible for Students:
The New King James Version (Tyndale House Publishers)

Lessons in Living
by Susan L. Taylor

Don't Block the Blessings: Revelations of a Lifetime
by Patti Labelle, Laura B. Randolph

A Woman After God's Own Heart
by Elizabeth George

A Plentiful Harvest: Creating Balance and Harmony Through the Seven Living Virtues
by Terrie Williams

Other Helpful Books

The 7 Lively Sins
How to Enjoy Your Life, Dammit
by Karen Salmansohn

Celebration of Discipline
by Richard Foster
(He also has a new book on prayer.)

Daily Word for Women: 365 Days of Love, Inspiration, and Guidance
written and edited by Colleen Zuck, Janie Wright, and Elaine Meyer

Life of the Beloved (chapter on *Broken*)
by Henri Nouwen

Make Each Day Your Masterpiece: Practical Wisdom for Living an Exceptional Life
by Michael Lynberg

The Artist's Way: A Spiritual Path to Higher Creativity
by Julia Cameron

The Celestine Prophecy
by James Redfield

Sacred Circles
by Robin Deen Carnes and Sally Craig

Sister to Sister Devotions for and from African-American Women
Suzan D. Johnson Cook, Editor

Writing from Life: Telling Your Soul's Story
by Susan Wittig Albert, Ph.D.

The Prayer of Jabez
by Bruce Wilkinson

You Can Heal Your Life
by Louise L. Hay

The Power of a Praying Wife
by Stormie Omartian and Michael Omartian

Souls of My Sisters
Dawn Marie Daniels and Candace Sandy, Editors

Networking Organizations

The AmASSI Center focuses on providing opportunities for diverse people of African descent to enhance their lives, community, and environment; to gain skills toward a healthy, affirmative, and prosperous life.
www.amassi.com

Black Communities AIDS Team
Leeds City Council, Health Unit, Selectapost 14, 2nd Fl.
Annex, Civic Hall, Leeds LS1 3AQ, 053-462431.

Blacks Educating Blacks about Sexual Health Issues (BEBASHI)
1233 Locust St. # 401
Philadelphia, PA 19107-5414
(215) 546-4140

Black HIV/AIDS Forum
AIDS Unit # 6003, Town Hall Extension,
Manchester M60 2JB.

Black Women's Health Imperative, the new name of the National Black
Women's Health Project, is a leading African-American health education, research, advocacy, and leadership development institution. Founded in 1983
by health activist Byllye Y. Avery, it has been a pioneer in promoting the empowerment of African-American women as educated health care consumers
and a strong voice for the improved health status of African-American
women. http://www.blackwomenshealth.org

Black Women's Network
Marva Smith Battle-Bey, chairperson
P.O. Box 56106
Los Angeles, CA 90056
FAX (323) 964-4003

California Black Women's Health Project
Emphasizing individual responsibility and interpersonal support, we seek to
improve the health of Black women and girls using a proactive approach.
http://www.cabwhp.org

Caribbean Women's Health Association
244 Utica Ave.
Brooklyn, NY 11213
(718) 826-2942

Haitian Coalition on AIDS
50 Court St. # 605
Brooklyn, NY 11201
(718) 855-7275

International Black Women's Network are women with a vision. We are
proactive and focused on each one of us helping the other achieve.
http://www.blackliving.net

Majority Action Committee
ACT-UP, Box 7932
New York, NY 10150

Men of Color AIDS Prevention
Office of Gay and Lesbian Health Issues, Department of Health,
125 Worth St. # 1100, Box 67,
New York, NY 10013
(212) 788-4310; FAX (212) 788-9661

National Association of African American Studies
Lemuel Berry, Jr., executive director
Morehead State University
Morehead, KY 40351
(606) 783-2650; FAX (606) 783-5046

National Association of Black Social Workers
Barbara Thomas, co-chair, National Conf. Committee
8436 W. McNichols Street
Detroit, MI 48221
(313) 862-6700; FAX (313) 862-6998

National Association of Black Women Entrepreneurs Inc.
Marilyn French-Hubbard, founder and meeting planner
P.O. Box 311299
Detroit, MI 48231
(313) 203-3379; FAX (248) 354-3793

National Association of Negro Business and Professional Women's Club
Sherelle Carper, National Convention Coordinator
1806 New Hampshire Avenue N.W.
Washington, DC 20009
(202) 483-4206; FAX (202) 462-7253

National Coalition of 100 Black Women
Diane Lloyd, Program Associate

38 West 32nd Street
New York, NY 10001
(212) 947-2196; FAX (212) 947-2477

National Task Force on AIDS Prevention
973 Market St. # 600
San Francisco, CA 94103 (415) 356-8100
FAX (415) 356-8103, (415) 356-8138
ntfap@aol.com

People of Color in Crisis
462 Bergen St.
Brooklyn, NY 11217
(718) 230-0770; FAX (718) 230-7582

People of Color Issues Committee, American Association of Physicians for
Human Rights
459 Fulton St. # 107, San Francisco, CA 94114
(415) 255-4547; (415) 255-4784 (fax)
gaylesmed@aol.com

Professional Women of Color
Tara Lawrence, president
P.O. Box 5196 New York, NY 10185
(212) 714-7190
www.pwcnetwork.org

Project Survival
1150 Griswold
Detroit, MI 48226,
(313) 961-2027, FAX (313) 961-0780

San Francisco Black Coalition on AIDS
1042 Divisadero St.
San Francisco, CA 94115-4409
(415) 346-2364; FAX (415) 346-6037
sfbcoa@earthlink.net

Acknowledgments

Special thanks to all my friends, family, and supporters.

To my husband, Abdeltif Tazi: You are my heart and have taught me so many valuable lessons in life. You are truly a servant of God. I thank God daily for blessing me with one of his very own angels. You have made so many rainy days sunny. Thank you for showing me how to love unconditionally. I never knew angels existed until I met you. My lessons in love are not finished yet, but I sure am glad God used you to teach it to me. I now realize that marriage is so much more than being together, sharing things, and looking cute. Through you I have learned that it's about being in each others' life to make each other better people. I love our differences, and I will always cherish your light!

Brenda Anderson (Mom)
You are beautiful! Thanks for bringing me into the world and thanks

for nurturing the talent within me and allowing me to be myself at all costs. Thanks for the sewing machine, the trumpet, and the video camera, for which you didn't have the money but that you sacrificed in hopes that I would always believe in myself. You have shown me so many ways to express myself. Thank you Mom. I love you.

Robert Anderson, Sr. (Dad)
I would not have made it this far had you not been a survivor of life and illness. Your personality and charm is amazing. I now know that God doesn't give us more than we can bear. It has been because you are strong that I have been able to witness God's mercy. I love you, Dad! You are my SUPERMAN!

Lillie Marie Green
You made summer wonderful. Thank you for loving me and teaching me how to speak. Who knew that one day I would have the opportunity to speak to the world? I will never forget the days of old. Those were truly the best times of my life. Thank you.

Robert Anderson, Jr.
You are an excellent brother. You have a lot of love and giving in your heart. Remember you are in the world to change the world. Thank you for always being brave!

Jennifer Jones
You have shown me so much of what it means to be committed. I thank God for your love and support. You let me know what it feel like to have a real sister in my life. Thanks for taking me back to my past so I can find my future. I love you!

Robert Anderson III
You are awesome! You are just like me (ha, ha).

Christopher Gaskins
My second brother, I love you! You are really going to bless a nation of people with your gift of song!

To all my aunts and uncles: Thanks for your kind words of love: Divolia Anderson, Karen Courman, Barbara Gaskins, Emma Green-Hines, Gloria Anderson, Gracie Baker, Melvin Gaskins, the Rev. George Melvin Gaskins, Jr., William and Louise Green, Kevin and Cathy Green, Andy and Joyce Anderson, Henry Gaskins, Bishop Paul Gaskins and Belinda, Rayford and Alice Gaskins, J.W. Gaskins, Leroy Gaskins, Reginald and Deborah Gaskins, Aunt Tess

Terrie Williams
I thank God for you! I respect you and I am grateful that God delivered you to me at Bowie State University in 1986. Your light has allowed me to see what it means to serve others and always give back. You have *taught* me a lot about what it means to believe in myself and stay strong!

Marie Williams
Thank you for always showing me that I can't go home again and that I must grow up. Thank you for watching over my life. You are a great godmother!

Patricia Anderson
Thanks for being so giving. I couldn't have asked God for a more thoughtful and loving mother.

Andrea, Tabitha, and Jacinta
Thanks for always being so sweet.

To the Tazi Family: Thank you for your support.
Chakib, Zoila, Redoune, Anna, Jawad, Najat.

Malika and Ahmed Tazi
Your light of love has brought four good men into the world. Thank you for always praying over their lives and the life of our entire family. When you come to visit you come to serve. You are always giving, and you are always sharing. That is the very essence of what God has called on all of us to be. Thank you for your wonderful light of love.

Marinel Lopez
I can see and feel your light from Atlanta, Georgia. Thanks for all your love and support.

Justin Anderson, Robert Anderson, III, Elisha Sutton, Shemonie King, Adam Tazi, Zakiyyah Hines, Jasmine Tazi, Kamar Tazi, Brittany Green, Eddie, Zachary Tazi, Takaheri Hines, Khalid Hines, Cameron Green.
Remember to never burn your bridges and always love, laugh, forgive, and give. My prayer is that you will be able to use this book as a reminder that God loves you and that you must always love and no matter what always pray you all have very bright future and you were born to make the world a better place. Know that I love you and I will always be praying over your lives.

My goddaughter *Ayah Tazi* you are the light of your mom and dad's life. I am so pleased to share in the call to raise you and to help make you the best woman you can possibly be. . . . My prayer for you is that you will always remember to believe that God is your guiding light. I love you! Remember to always put God first!

Thank you cousins. I love you all. . . . Annette Brown, Jocelyn Brown, Ray Gaskins, Jr., LaRita Gaskins, Kim Gaskins, Kayswanna Brown, Dion, Pete Buckell, Naja Gaskins Jonathan, Paul and Jason Gaskins, Rudy Gaskins, Ngosi Gaskins, Nia Gaskins, David Hines, Shevon

Courman, Natalie Hines, William K. Green III, Sharie Courman, Rodney Gaskins, J.W. Gaskins, Leroy Gaskins, Mark Anthony Gaskins, Tianna Hodgson, Patrick Hodgson, Trinna Gaskins, Bertrum Gaskins, Reggie and Deborah Gaskins and family.

Much love to all of my Gaskins, Anderson, Tazi, and the Green family. May we continue to share our lives with the world and, hopefully, make the world a better place.

Heavenly Powell
You are my Baby SISTAH. I admire the woman you are and the woman you are growing to be. You are awesome!

Uncle Rock and Aunt Barbara
I love you. Thanks for seeing me in all times and loving at all times.

Tridina Anderson
You made growing up fun.

To all my special friends:

Chalyce Noel-Williams
You are my RD light. You have brought so much joy to my life. Thanks for pushing me when I was afraid.

Joy Williams and family
May God continue to use you to inspire others as you have done for me. I believe in you and I admire your strength.

Zelda Umana
I love you and have been truly blessed by your friendship.

D.G. Wilson-Davis
What can I say about a woman who has brought lots of love, gentleness, and compassion into my life. From one survivor to the next, you are my angel.

Debra Coiffeur
Thank you for showing me mad love.

Gretta Jackson
Your energy is impeccable I love you and I admire your way to love!

Giselle Jackson
Thank you for making me part of your life. I miss you like mad!

Jimmy and Cheryl Lane-Lewis
Thanks for lending me your home and thanks for always praying for my life. You are the sister and brother God gave me as a gift.

Albert and Marie Davis
I love you. Thanks for taking me in as your daughter.

Barbara McFarland
You are the best. Barbara, your light inspired me to stay on course on the trip to Atlantic City when my life was changing.

Reverend Ruth Travis
You gave me a lot of encouragement. Thanks for praying for me.

Brenda Carter
You are such an inspiration. Thanks for seeing the light that lives inside of me.

Terry Moore
Thank you for helping me remember that I am sane (ha, ha).

Vickie Cowan
Thanks for finding me and making me feel special.

Jacqueline Ramos
You have saved, and must continue to save, the lives of women across Westchester. Thanks for working on the behalf of the survivors of Westchester.

Lisa Pantano and Erin McMahon
Your hope in my success really helped me get through. Thanks for your love and always listening. You are my dynamic duo.

Joyce Kelly
You have taught me the new meaning of being dedicated to the service of the Lord. Thanks for crying with me and allowing me to tell you my happy and painful times.

Jennifer Simpson
Thank you for always sharing what you see in me and making me live up to my potential.

Shella Lieberman
Thanks for helping me see that you don't have to lose your life in order to share your life. You are a true emerald in my life. I love you, Steven. Thank you, Kenny.

Kevin and Kecia Palmer Cousins
We met because we have something to give to one another. I gave you

aerobics; you gave me the publishing world. You are very special to me. Kevin, I love doing aerobics with you!

Gail Perry
Love you. Thanks for sharing your aunts with me. They are so special and so are you.

My attorney Vernon Slaughter and his assistant Dion
Thank you for believing in someone you have never seen. You have empowered me beyond words. Hurry up and write your book, Vernon.

Darwin Laws
You are an excellent single dad and a great friend. Thank you for just being a good listener, and please don't write my untold story (ha, ha).

Liz, Chris, and Hunter Paul
My extended family, thanks for being such good friends.

Shakuwra, Samiyrah, and Yaasmin
Thanks for always sharing your life with me. My life is brighter with you in it!

Samara, Tracey and Monique
My three sisters, I love you and may heaven continue to smile on you with light of love. Samara, congratulations on Café Ellis!

Fred Staton
Thank you for always showing me care.

Jakki Taylor
I think you are awesome!

ACKNOWLEDGMENTS

Reverend and Mrs. Jones
Thank you for always opening your home to me and my family. Thanks for the example of how a Christian home works and being Christ-like.

Leslie and Kenny
I really feel like you are my sistah and brotha. Thanks for loving my family and always being so giving. Thanks for adopting Amir as your nephew. (ha, ha)

Star Jones
Thanks for giving me my first big national television break. You gave me the opportunity to inspire the world to stay fit.

Sonya Watkins
You are always in my heart. I can't wait until you believe what I can see. I am proud of you.

Deborah Dorsey
You are still my big sister.

Leon Davis
Your love and inspiration helped me to be the woman I am. Thanks for believing that I could live with a diagnosis of cancer. Thanks for believing in my dreams. You are hard working, caring, strong, talented, and intelligent. Your light will always shine bright in my life—and the lives of so many others!

Claudia Edwards
Thanks for making me part of your spiritual life. Greater Centennial is a great church and you are great.

Sister David
Your life has made my life turn from silver to gold. I am glad God used you to help me understand his purpose and promise. On Friday 8:30 P.M. my life was changed forever. Thanks for ushering me into the presence of the Lord!

Tracey Adams
You are very special to me!

Zoila Figueroa
Thanks for allowing God to use you as my angel.

Reverend Darrin Moore
Thank you for the awesome examples of great leadership.

Mark Brown
You are one of the most amazing speakers I have ever heard. Thank you for being a great example.

Dr. Arthur
Thanks for being so gentle and kind. Please continue to help save lives.

Bertina Travis
Thanks for always having an open-door policy. Your way of sharing hospitality food and laughter made me believe God existed.

Catherine Williams
Your love gave me hope.

Brenda Davis
Thank you for always caring.

Wendy Johnson
Thanks for remembering our past on the children's choir and in school and embracing our future as friends. Your prayer helped me remember that I can still be!

Vera Chesely and the Office of Media Operations
Thanks for showing me that you believed in my ability to be a television personality. I am blessed to have your light live in my heart.

Dr. Nedd Gaskins, Ida Brandon, and Jean Wicks
Thanks for believing in me.

Delores Worsham
Thanks for the gift of song. You are a morning angel. May God bless you all the days of your life.

Terry Chapman
Thank you for always making me feel like I am never alone.

Kim Anderson
Don't forget the world needs your talent. You are an amazing woman and I know that your life is going to change the lives of so many others. Your gift of song is amazing. Eddie and Justin are growing to be great men because of their great mother.

Alan Gansberg
Thanks for all the great advice as an artist. . . . Your time and effort was most appreciated.

Sarah Burns
Congratulations on being a healer for your family. You are a diamond!

Monique Brown McKenzie
Thank you for seeing the need for the world to hear my story. I have watched you, as founder and CEO of the Professional Women of Color, bring hundreds of Women of Color together in hopes that we can believe that we have a place in corporate and not-so-corporate America. I am proud to be affiliated with someone who not only cares about women of color but cares about the need for us to be heard. Congratulations on your current book and thanks again for caring and seeing the need for my story to be told. May God continue to shine his light on your life and bless your family with the spirit to continue to change the universe just as you have changed mine.

Thank you *Barbara Lowenstein* and *Norman Kurz,* from Lowenstein and Associates. Barbara, you and Norman make a great team.

Tonya White
Your giving spirit is a great example to us all. Thanks for your awesome light! Me and my family are blessed to have you in our lives.

Monique Boone
You are one strong woman. I am so glad we are friends.

Towanda Hayes
I am so proud to have you as my friend. I am inspired by your strength to endure heartache. Remember to always trust that God has something powerful in store for your life and he truly is not finished with you yet!

Joan Greene
You are so beautiful. I really enjoy watching how graceful and talented you are with kids. Thanks for assuring me that I can have a baby, and, more importantly, sharing my experience of being a stay-at-home mom.

Filomena Sousa

You came into my life at the perfect time. You have the gift of painting that must be shared with the world. Thanks for the gift of hope and prayer!

Christine Zika of The Berkley Publishing Group

Thanks for seeing me through my rough times and having a sensitive ear toward my challenge in the midst of a blessing. You have made this rocky road smooth.

Mayer Elementary, Hillcrest Heights Elementary, Silver Hill Elementary, Andrew Jackson Junior High, Herring Run Junior High, Lake Clifton Senior High, College of Notre Dame, Bowie State University

YMCA of Harlem

Thank you for embracing the spirit of survivorship.

FORCE—Jeff Berman

I sometimes cry when I think of your vision, because, had it not been for your vision for FORCE in Harlem, I would not have been blessed with my extended family.

Glorie Browne, Wylene Nebblett, Marie Waldron, Eula Colbert, Joanne Hill, Diana Augustus, Asha Golliher, Patricia Hipplewith, Barbara Wane, Vanessa Green, Priscilla Romaine, Valerie Gunn, Janelle Farris, Ellen Pearson, Bahijah St. Louis, Linnette General, Phyllis Gomez, Mildred Strawter

I'm glad God gave us something in common because of all of you I am a better woman . . . you are true survivors in every sense of the word.

ACKNOWLEDGMENTS

Park Avenue Imaging
Dr. V thank you for unconditionally caring about so many women who need your care. You're the best!

Bowie State University
You are the number-one HBCU in all the world. Keep changing the lives of inner city youth. You definitely changed mine.

Professional Women of Color
For showing me that women can get together and embrace each other's power to succeed.

Manhattan College family and students
Shawn Ladda, thank you for empowering me. You believed in me and that I will never forget.

The Whosoeverwill Church of God in Christ
Thank you for making my wedding memorable.

American Cancer Society of White Plains
Thanks for helping me get back and forth to chemo. I met some awesome people.

Support Connection of Yorktown Heights
I didn't have the money to get my first mammogram and you supplied me with an excellent doctor, Dr. V. He not only helped me understand my mammogram, but I never met a more gentle doctor in all my life. Thank you and thanks for serving so many women. Dr. V, you're the best.

YWCA of Yonkers staff and friends
You helped me get my first start at becoming a survivor in the fitness world. Thank you, Patricia Sadler.

YWCA of White Plains
May you continue to be dedicated to the lives of those still trapped in the pain of racism.

YMCA of Mount Vernon family, Vann Barnes, Lenny Dixon
Your dedication to fitness kept me inspired.

Brooklyn Tabernacle
Your light in the midst of a hectic city allowed me to see that God is everywhere. I learned about having a personal relationship with God through you.

Eastern United Methodist Church
You are my beginning and I am eternally grateful.

To all my *Reader's Digest* family, you are the BEST!

Toastmasters family
Thanks for teaching me how to perfect my speaking ability.

Faith in Action
Your prayers got me through. Thank you, Joyce.

Greater Centennial A.M.E.
I am proud of you, and I am proud to be part of your family.

ACKNOWLEDGMENTS

Bethel A.M.E. of Baltimore
Thank you, Reverend Reid. Your ministry helped me Believe!

Joan Sheehy, Elizabeth Seeds, Vanda Nunes, Cynthia DiPietro, Richard Clark, Jason Tuthill, Theresa McNiff, Rosemarie Carabajal, Sandy Lancton, Cindy Foley, Debra Nielsen, Roy Lindo, Eugene Eskildsen, Richard Fitzgerald, Randy Scheller, William Magill, Laura Russo, Barbara Deem, Fina Escusa, Amy Rabadi, Norma Jean-Jacques, Tina Porter, Stella Nahmias, Yadira Jankowsi, Stephanie Kiluk, Mary Adamovic, All of the Ya Ya Sistahood, Ruth Grundler, Jon Rivera, Debbie Scherer, Richard Prejs, Christine Schneyman, Christine Zarrella, Marcus Griffith, Howard, Stevenson, Bob Gorun.

Small World Day Care Facility
Thank you for taking care of my child in such an awesome way. The children of Yonkers have been blessed by your dedication and hard work. Thank you, Ms. Terry, Ms. Lois, and Ms. Gina!

To White Plains Hospital
You have extended your care to accommodate the survivors of tomorrow thank you for caring about cancer amongst all people.

Dr. Bavaro
You are the best doctor. Your constant lines of communication and your personal touch are hard to find these days. Thank you for being so proactive in my life. Dr. Leikin, Stephanie, Dana, and your entire support team have really made my challenge easy.

Rachel Alexander and Mother Edith
God sent you as my angels at the perfect time. I love you both.

Credits and Permissions